WHAT'S NEXT,
LORD?

A YOUNG NURSE ADJUSTS TO
WORKING WITH EPILEPTICS

REBEKAH HANSON WILSON

TABLE OF CONTENTS

—◦◦◦—

Chapter 1

JUST ANOTHER DAY

I t seemed like just another ordinary day when Miss Bea Jenkins arrived at Cottage Two of the Crystal Colony in River Ridge, Minnesota on a beautiful spring morning in 1924. Tossing her bag onto the desk in the Nurses' Office, she glanced into the mirror above the sink to straighten the small, white, heavily starched and ruffled, organdy cap which perched atop her strawberry blond curls like a delicate, exotic bird sitting on its' nest. A brief feeling of pride welled up within her as she noted the narrow, blue, velvet ribbon across one edge of the cap, indicating to anyone who understood the symbolism of it that she was now a Graduate Nurse.

Giving her hair a pat to see if all the hair pins and combs were in place, she crossed the hall and unlocked the door into J-Ward where she had been assigned to work when she came here a few days ago. She was already getting into the routine of the ward.

The first order of the day for her was to check each of the inmates for new symptoms and/or injuries since she had seen them the day before. As she circulated about the ward, observing each person and answering questions put to her by the attendants, the only thing that seemed to be unusual was that Jack Ival seemed to be more agitated than usual, pacing about and stopping at each window and door to try to find a way to escape.

Some high-level inmates were busy making beds in the large dormitory on the second floor where their charges slept in long rows of narrow beds. The inmates were gender segregated in their living quarters, so there were only men and boys in this building. Other workers were assisting the more handicapped people to get cleaned up, dressed, and to the breakfast tables in the basement, where they sat in a row on long benches, hooked by a strap to their belts and then to the wall behind them. The noise was always at a high pitch during this time. Bea wondered if she would ever get used to it.

Nothing in nurse's training had prepared her for this kind of setting. For one thing, she had been instructed here to refer to the patients as, "Inmates." This sounded to her as if they were all considered to be criminals, confined to a prison of some kind. That just hit her the wrong way.

Another thing which was difficult to adjust to was that many of the inmates could not speak in normal words. Most of them made some kind of unique verbalizations. She was beginning to recognize Jimmy's squawk, Bobby's calf's bellow imitation. Arther's hawk like cry, and Henry's grunts. Many of the other sounds she had not sorted out yet, but they were all tuned up this morning, like a special kind of orchestra, each adding their own point and counterpoint to the rhythm of their symphony.

Something else which she had not really been prepared for was the physical appearance of many of the inmates. They were the ones who had been brought here shortly after birth on the advice of the doctors who had delivered them because they were suffering from multiple handicaps. They had been hidden away from the general public. Their parents rarely or never came to visit and siblings and other extended family members may not have even known of their existence. Many were brain damaged, with varying levels of mentality. Some were grotesque in physical appearance, with tortured bodies and facial distortions. Many had behaviors, which were not acceptable in *polite society,* biting, hitting, drooling, spitting, self abuse, pacing, rocking, screaming, eating non-edibles, wetting and dirtying themselves, smearing or stealing food, and breaking furniture and other items in their environment.

Bea was repulsed by some of them and hesitated to even touch them because of these deformities and behaviors. She had great admiration for the caregivers who were able to give them hugs and care for them on a very intimate level for many hours at a time. She felt somewhat guilty because of her own feelings of fear and revulsion toward them. The words of Jesus came to her as she watched the scene before her.

> ***"Inasmuch as ye did it to one of the least of these my brethren, ye did it to me."***
> ***(Matthew 25:40)***

She didn't think she would ever be able to get used to the odors of this place either. Bea had discovered early in nurses' training that she had a special "gift" of smell. Her nose seemed to be much more sensitive than other people's. There were times when this had been a good thing, like when she found that she was able to diagnose such illnesses and Diabetes or Smallpox just by being in close proximity to a patient. At other times, it was a definite trial for her to have a keen sense of smell because in this work there were many things which gave off decidedly offensive odors.

There were also many higher functioning inmates living at the colony only because they were slow learners or because they had uncontrolled epilepsy of one form or another. Many of these epileptics were highly intelligent. This group of higher functioning inmates worked right along with the other caregivers, helping to care for the lower level inmates and working in the kitchen, farm, grounds, and laundry. Bea had already found out that if one inmate wanted to insult another, they called them a "Low Grade." This never failed to get their hackles up. Some of these more intelligent inmates had a history of criminal and/or anti-social behaviors. Bea had been warned to be careful around them because of this.

Suddenly, the outside door swung open and one of the farm workers burst in, accompanied by Glenn Schubert, a tall, well built, very intelligent inmate. Glen had curly, blond hair with blond eyebrows and lashes. He was living at the colony only because he had uncontrolled epilepsy.

More than fifty percent of the inmates suffered from epilepsy of some form or another, which is why Crystal Colony was usually referred to as the "Epilepsy Colony."

The Colony was pretty much self sufficient and self-supporting. They had a farm, an orchard, a dairy, a bakery, a school, and a small infirmary. Most of the staff lived on campus in small houses or apartments. Glenn was actually more intelligent and a better farmer than most of the paid attendants with whom he worked.

Old Dr. Irwin often said, "The keys to this place are in the wrong hands. The inmates have more sense than the staff."

Glenn headed straight for Bea and stopped directly before her, with his legs spread wide, while gesturing wildly with his hands.

"We need you in the barn right away," he commanded. "Muley is sick and we need a nurse to help us."

Bea had no idea who Muley was, but Glenn's tone and stance convinced her that she had to respond to his demands without hesitation. She simply followed him and the farm attendant out the door and locked it behind her as they ran together. Matching his long strides with lengthy ones of her own they ran toward the barn yard. Her white uniform skirt flapped about her legs, her delicate cap bounced around on her head, as if about to take flight. The closer they got to the barn, the louder she heard a strange sound she had never heard before. It was a mixture of moaning, screaming, and bawling. She figured that it must be the uttering of an inmate with whom she had not yet come into contact. One thing that was certain. That individual was in a lot of pain.

When they entered the barn, she observed several men standing in one of the stalls, looking down at something on the floor. The men parted to let her and Glen through and Bea let out a surprised,

"What the —-?

There on the stall floor on the hay lay a large, black mule on his back, his legs pointing strait skyward. When he saw her, his cries became louder, almost deafening. His eyes rolled about and his belly was swollen so large that it seemed it would blow up in her face.

"He ate too much fresh green grass and foundered!" Glenn yelled over the din. I've called for the vet, but he isn't available. We need to take his temperature and then try to figure out how to help him."

This was a situation that Bea had heard of, having been raised on her grandparents' farm, but had never had personal experience with.

Bea stared wide eyed at Glenn in disbelief.

"I don't know how to take a mule's temperature," she hollered back.

"You just do it like you do a person," Glenn screamed, as he took a large glass thermometer from a leather case on a shelf and handed it to her with some Vaseline

Bea stood over the mule, shaking her head.

"Why can't you do it?" she asked.

"I have to hold his head to calm him while you do it," he answered. "I'm the only one he trusts around here."

The men standing around in a circle were all nodding in agreement as Muley continued to let out his head splitting caterwauling.

"Anything to stop this awful noise," muttered Bea to herself as she reached for the thermometer. "They certainly didn't tell me this would be one of my jobs here."

She coated the thermometer well with the lubricant and eased around to the business end of the mule as Glenn took its head in his lap and gently stroked it while murmuring soothing sounds into its long ear. One of the farm attendants stood to the side, holding Muley's tail.

This is the craziest thing I have ever been involved with in my life, thought Bea, as she cautiously brought the thermometer toward the animal's anal sphincter. *Oh well, here goes.*

The tip of the thermometer slid with a little pop through the aperture, and then, with explosive force, it flew out of her hand like a rocket across the stall and out the barn door, followed by a huge stream of liquid, green excrement. Muley let out a beller and then a groan.

Bea was not quick enough to get out of the way, so her hand and forearm were covered with the stuff. She screamed like she had been shot and her legs pumped up and down, running in place without actually going anywhere. She couldn't stop screaming and her legs went on pumping until one of the farm attendants put his hands on her waist from behind, guiding her out of the barn to the horse trough where he washed her hand and arm, gently calming her with soft words of thanks.

All the men in the barn were laughing so hard that some of them had tears running down their faces and some were rolling around in the hay holding their sides.

Muley turned on his side and became suddenly silent, his eyes closed and he began to snore softly. Glenn kissed the mule on the top of his head and laid it on the straw.

When Glenn came through the barn door, he strolled over to Bea, with a shy grin on his face and asked,

"Are you all right, Miss?"

"No thanks to you!" she responded angrily and then began to cry.

He put his arms around her and patted her gently on the back.

"I'm sorry," he responded. "I guess I should have known that would happen. Please forgive me." adding,

"You sure did help old Muley though."

The barnyard was quiet as Bea stood weeping into Glenn's shoulder.

Suddenly, the silence was broken with the sound of squealing tires and the roar of an engine. Around the corner of the corn crib careened a shiny new black, 1924, Packard sedan. It shot across the barnyard, up over the dike beside the pond behind the barn, and flew through the air, landing on its side in the shallow water, slowly settling into the mud on the bottom. All the windows were rolled up on the car and the faces of several inmates could be identified looking blandly out the windows above the water line.

Victor Sando peered out with his wide-eyed, blank expressionless gaze from the back window, munching slowly and mechanically on a piece of toast spread with peanut butter, as if this was not an unusual place for him to eat a morning snack. The only occupant of the vehicle who seemed in the least concerned was the driver, Jack Ival, who had somehow managed to make an escape from J-Ward and had taken a few friends along for a ride in the new automobile belonging to Crystal Colony's administrator, Dr. Bruce Anderson. Jack was trying frantically to extricate himself from the confines of the half submerged vehicle but was having a tough time getting untangled from the arms and legs of his hapless passengers. He was a tall, wiry, not very well coordinated young man.

By this time the men who had been laughing themselves silly in the barn were all standing atop the dike, scratching their heads trying to solve this new problem. They waded into the water, opened the car doors on the passenger's side, and pulled the inmates out, handing them one to the other until they were all safe on dry land. Attendants from the ward had arrived and helped herd the adventurers back to the locked building.

Jack was pretty docile after all the excitement and went along with no more rebellion. Actually, he looked a little sheepish as he trudged along with the others. Everyone knew that he was going to be headed for the *Coop* and/or *Hydro*.

The Coop was what the inmates and some of the staff called the seclusion room. This was a room with padded walls and floors, no windows, one wire screen covered, light bulb on the ceiling, a toilet and a bare mattress. A screen covered peephole in the heavy steel door allowed staff members to observe the occupant. Inmates were placed in this room to calm down when their behaviors became too difficult for the staff to control. The inmate would be left there for hours or days, depending on how they responded.

Everyone referred to the Hydrotherapy Department, as *Hydro*. When an inmate was taken there, they were subjected to one or more of the treatments provided.

One treatment was to strip the person of their clothes and spray them with alternating streams of very warm and very cold water.

Another treatment was to place them, naked, into a tub of warm water, their bodies total submerged except for their head, which stuck out of a canvas covering over the top of the tub. This covering was fastened to the tub so that it was impossible to get out without help.

The third experience which an inmate might experience in *Hydro*, was to be stripped of clothing and wrapped like a mummy with cold wet sheets, then swaddled in wool blankets and laid on a hard table, unable to move. Their body heat would slowly warm them up.

The effect of all of these procedures was supposed to calm a person who was upset, agitated, or aggressive. Amazingly, it usually worked, no matter how low the person's mental function.

Dr. Anderson had arrived on the scene at the pond, and was having his own private nervous breakdown over the drowning of his beautiful new car. His scalp had habit of moving back and forth rapidly from front to back when he was disturbed and his thick, white hair moved with great vigor as he wrung his plump, pink hands together and made strange sounds under his breath.

Everyone was glancing out the side of their eyes at Dr. Anderson, wondering whose heads were going to roll for this incident.

Bea had been standing back observing this new fiasco. She turned to Glenn with a bewildered look and asked, "Is it always like this around here?"

A slow grin spread across his sun tanned face as he answered, "Oh, more or less."

Shaking her head, Bea walked slowly back to the J-Ward, where everything had returned to a semblance of order.

At this point, she decided to retreat to the Nurses' Office to do some documenting and have a quiet cup of coffee.

The door to the office was standing open when she arrived there and two other staff nurses; Miss Janis, a petite, awkward, young woman who would never be called pretty, and middle-aged, dark haired, kindly, Mrs. Kelly were sitting at desks writing and drinking coffee. Bea greeted them and filled them in on the happenings of the morning while she scrubbed her arms and hands with surgical soap at the sink.

A glance in the mirror told Bea that her beautiful new cap had been knocked askew and looked as if it was about to make a quick escape. As the other nurses laughed at her description of her morning, she looked for her bag to find a comb and some hairpins to try to repair some of her dishevelment. The bag was nowhere to be found.

"Now what," she said with great exasperation. "I know I put that thing right here on this desk."

The three of them searched the office thoroughly, but came up empty handed.

Are you sure you closed the door tightly when you left the office this morning?" Mrs. Kelly asked. "Sometimes it doesn't lock if you don't close it firmly."

By this time, Bea was almost at the point of emotional exhaustion.

"How much is a nurse expected to go through in one morning, anyway?" she asked.

She sat down in a chair and buried her head on her arms which she had folded on the desk before her.

"This is just too much. Now what am I going to do?"

"Don't worry, Albert probably has it. He's always checking this office to see if he can get in," consoled Miss Janis, with a pat on Bea's back.

"Come on, Kelly, let's go have a talk with Ol' Albert."

The two left Bea in the office as they went together to find Albert, a high functioning, sticky fingered, inmate whose room was next door to the nurses' office. He denied having anything to do with the bag, so they took him with them back to the scene of the crime so he could see how upset the pretty new nurse was. They knew that he was a kind hearted thief. When he saw how distraught Bea was he said that he would try to find the bag and quickly returned with it, with everything still inside.

The rest of the day was uneventful. All the documentation was done and the staff got everything back into shape on the ward, but Bea was totally exhausted when seven o'clock came and she could go to her apartment to collapse. Twelve hour shifts were the rule of thumb at the Colony and that is a long time to spend in such a stimulating atmosphere.

Chapter 2

THE INVITATION

A s Bea lay on her bed in her apartment, she decided to read the mail which had come for her that day. The first letter she picked up had the familiar handwriting of Grandmother Stretch on the front. But, as she began to tear open the envelope, she noticed that the other envelope looked more intriguing. It was light lavender, with white trim and the address was written in some kind of fancy lettering. The return address was that of a new acquaintance she had met at a quilting bee last week. Mrs. Patricia Wilkey was a Fine Arts teacher at the Normal School nearby. (Normal Schools were what they called colleges for the training of aspiring teachers.)

Inside that envelope was an invitation to a dinner party at the Wilkey home on the very next evening. Bea knew already that the Wilkey's had a reputation for interesting, unique dinner parties, though she had never imagined that she would ever be invited to one.

Dr. Robert Wilkey was also a professor at the Normal School. He was the son of a British aristocrat who had been a famous Egyptologist. One of Dr. Wilkey's uncles had been a bachelor and a railroad baron and had left his fortune to Robert. The professor taught Ancient History, and was reputed to be one of the most boring instructors on campus.

Bea felt that it was a real honor to be invited to a dinner party at the Wilkey home. She figured that only the highly educated and more artsy members of the community would be invited there. Tomorrow would be her first day off since completing her orientation at the Colony and she would not have to return to work until seven o'clock on Saturday night. That would be the beginning of her ten night stretch on the "hoot owl shift."

Lying there contemplating the possibilities and what she might wear to such a prestigious event, someone called to her from the hallway, saying that she had a telephone call. She dragged herself up and padded down the hall in her bedroom slippers to the communal telephone.

"This is Miss Jenkins," she said into the instrument on the wall.

The familiar voice of her cousin, Alan Ward answered.

"Hi, cousin. How have you been doing in your new job?"

"Don't ask," she answered.

"This has been an indescribable day and I have to digest it for awhile before I'll be ready to tell you about it. Is everything alright with you and yours?"

"Natalie has a cold and Lena is teething again, but otherwise, we're just fine," he answered.

"I just called to tell you that I think I've made inroads into the intelligentsia set. Lydia and I have been invited to a dinner party at the home of Dr. and Mrs. Robert Wilkey tomorrow evening. Isn't that smashing?"

"That's wonderful," Bea replied. I just received an invitation to that dinner party, too. When did our family become high classed enough to be a part of that group? You must be making a fine impression on the faculty at the Normal

School since you started teaching there. Are you planning to go?"

"We sure are. They even invited us to bring the children. It could be an interesting evening all right."

Bea took a couple of seconds to assimilate this bit of news.

"That seems rather strange," she said, "a grown up party, and inviting small children to attend. That really does sound unusual. It sounds more like a family party with Grandmother and Grandfather and aunts and uncles and cousins. Oh, well, I guess they know what they're doing. Do you know how we're suppose to dress for one of these affairs?"

Alan's deep chuckle bubbled over the phone as he answered.

"Leave it to a woman to think of what to wear before considering anything else. That was the first question Lydia asked, too. I presume you should not wear your nurse's uniform, nor I my overalls. Let's just dress as if we were going to church on Sunday. That'll probably be the best. Would you like for us to take you with us in our surrey?"

"Yes. Thank you." answered Bea. "I'll be ready at six-fifteen."

"Great," responded Alan. "We'll see you then. Good-by now."

As Bea returned to her apartment she had a little more bounce in her step. But when she looked at her bed it seemed pretty inviting. With a deep sigh, she went to her wardrobe instead to look at her clothing to try to decide just what she should wear for the upcoming dinner party.

Then it dawned on her that she should be thinking of something else. Her hair would have to be washed tonight if it was to be looking its' best when she was seen in the company of such important hosts. Grandmother Stretch had always taught her that it is dangerous for a woman to go outside into the fresh air less than twenty-four hours after washing her hair or she would be taking the risk of getting a cold or quinsy. Even though Bea thought that this was pure superstition, she had been conditioned to abide by this rule. If she didn't wash her hair tonight, it wouldn't be safe to go to the party on Friday evening, because twenty-four hours would not have passed yet. So she made preparations to begin this task. Her hair was too long and thick to wash in the bathroom lavatory, so she filled the dish pan in the kitchen sink and washed and rinsed it there. She finished the job with a vinegar rinse, another of Grandmother Stretch's lessons. The vinegar was suppose to neutralize the shampoo and leave the hair shining.

When Bea had complained that the vinegar left her hair smelling like a cider press, her grandmother had replied,

"A few drops of vanilla on your wrists and behind your ears will take care of that."

Then she had added a phrase with which Bea would become very familiar as she grew into young womanhood "Anything to be beautiful," she had stated.

That was that.

After her hair was washed and rinsed, the next step was to wave and curl it. Combing all the tangles out, she pressed finger waves into the hair around the top and sides of her head, keeping them in place with combs and special clips. Next, she got out the rags. These were strips of cotton cloth, torn from an old sheet. She carefully wound strands of the hair around her face and shoulders on the rags and tied the ends to keep the curls in place.

She had been tempted lately to get her hair bobbed in the newest fashion, since it was a hard and fast rule that nurses must keep their hair up off their collar when in uniform. It would be so much easier to have short hair, but Grandmother Stretch had some very firm convictions in the area of the length of a woman's hair. She would click her tongue whenever she saw a woman with short hair and quote from the Bible.

"If a woman have long hair,
it is a glory to her?"
(1st Corinthians 10:15)

So, to keep the peace in the family, Bea continued to deal with the long locks. She was frequently complemented on her hair and knew that it was one of her best features.

By the time this labor intensive grooming chore was taken care of, Bea had begun to feel hungry. She had skipped supper so she could be alone and rest. She remembered the cheese in the icebox and the crackers in the cupboard. That sounded pretty good by now, so she crunched on them with an apple while she read her Bible and wrote in her journal. While she ate and wrote she found her eyelids drooping and her pen trailing off the edge of the page a couple of times before she put it all away. She had barely lain down on the bed before she was sound asleep. She didn't even feel the hardware on her head or remember that she hadn't yet read her grandmother's letter.

Chapter 3

INCIDENT IN THE TUNNEL

F riday dawned gray and overcast with the sound of thunder off in the distance. Bea would have loved nothing better than to remain snuggled in her bed for the entire morning, reading her new book, <u>The White Flag</u>, by her favorite author, Gene Stratton Porter, but she knew that she had to get her dirty uniforms, towels, and bedding over to the laundry building before nine o'clock on Friday mornings or they would not get washed and ironed in time to have them by Tuesday morning. Most of the laundry workers were inmates of the Colony, but she had been told that they did a wonderful job.

Before doing anything else though, she read a chapter in the <u>Bible</u> and then enjoyed Grandmother Stretch's letter. It was filled with news about Grandfather's lumbago and a nosy neighbor who was forever listening in on phone calls on the party line. Grandmother said that she had been praying for added grace and patience in dealing with the woman. This brought a smile to Bea. It made her think that even old Christians need to pray for help in dealing with little everyday problems.

Returning the letter to the envelope, she made a mental note to write back to her grandparents later in the day.

She dressed quickly in her sky blue gingham dress which was sprinkled with images of small yellow and white daisies and, stuffing her dirty laundry into the canvas bag marked with her name she ran down the back stairs to the Staff Recreation Room in the basement of the building. After bolting down a fresh baked muffin with apple butter and a glass of cold milk she found in the staff ice box, she headed for the underground tunnel, connecting all the buildings of the colony. She had only been in the tunnel once before and the thought of it wasn't pleasant. She wouldn't even have opted to go that way, except that the rain had arrived in earnest and she did not wish to go out into that deluge.

The tunnel system was made up of underground concrete hallways lighted with opaque skylights every fifty yards or so and a bare twenty-five watt light bulb hanging from the ceiling half way between every two skylights.

There were signs painted on the walls directing one to whatever building they were looking for, but it was easy to get turned around down there because it was so dimly lit and there were few landmarks to give a hint in what direction one was traveling.

The tunnel had two main functions. First, it was used to house water and steam pipes, which led from the power and water plant building to all the buildings on the grounds. This supplied hot and cold water and hot steam for heat in the winter. Secondly, the tunnel was used in cold or rainy weather for staff and inmates to move from one building to another without getting wet or cold. This was great during the cold, snowy winters in Minnesota.

The down side of this was that the pipes kept the tunnel hot in all kinds of weather. This was fine in the winter, but created a sauna like atmosphere in warm weather. Although there were ventilators every one hundred yards to let in fresh air from the outside, the atmosphere in the tunnel was always stale and fetid, especially on hot, humid days.

Bea had walked only about twenty yards along the tunnel when she heard weird noises behind her. Looking over her shoulder, she saw several shadowy figures moving along behind her. Creatures with misshapen bodies, deformed faces, ungainly gaits and animalistic noises came slowly through the gloom. It felt to her as if she were living in a waking nightmare. She was not yet desensitized to the sights, sounds, and especially the smells of this place. Suddenly she realized that the staff must be taking the inmates through the tunnel to the school building for their daily training classes because of the rain on the outside. She hurried along in front of them, not wanting to be caught in the crush and half afraid of what the inmates might do if they got too close to her since she was an unfamiliar person in their environment.

As she came to the next junction in the tunnel, she read the sign on the wall with an arrow pointing to the left which read, LAUNDRY, WAREHOUSE & BOILER ROOM. She turned following the arrow until she saw another sign saying, LAUNDRY.

By this time Bea had left the noisy, lumbering hoard far behind and she breathed a sigh of relief as she started up the ramp in that direction.

Then, she saw something which really frightened her. About ten yards up the ramp something large was on the floor. It was moving about in a strange way, and making guttural sounds.

She stopped to debate the most safe and intelligent action to take next. *It might be some kind of animal that got down here some way,* she thought. She was afraid to go closer to it for fear of being attacked, but she did not want to retrace her steps toward the sights and sounds of the crowd behind her either. She just stood there, staring into the semi-darkness ahead and watching the movements of the thing, which blocked her path.

"Lord, help me," she breathed.

As she stood, contemplating what her next move should be, she heard a new sound coming from the thing ahead. It sounded like someone choking. Cautiously, step by hesitant step, she began to move toward the thing on the ramp. She knew that she had to do something eventually, and that the writhing mass ahead of her did not seem to notice that she was there. As she drew closer to it and her eyes became more adjusted to the dim light, she realized that what she was observing was a person. She quickened her pace and approached the body on the floor.

"Oh no!" she gasped, as she got a good look. "It's Glenn, and he's having a seizure."

Her laundry bag dropped to the cement floor of the tunnel as she knelt to turn him onto his side. He seemed to be choking and she looked around for something to place between his teeth. The only thing she could think of was her dirty laundry. She retrieved a washcloth from the bag. Wrapping it around one of the combs she took from her hair, she forced the contraption gently between his teeth.

Blood oozed from between his lips indicating that he had probably already bitten his tongue. He had evidently hit his head when he fell in the convulsion and the back of his head was bleeding profusely. She used a folded towel to place under his head and another to place pressure over the gaping wound. She had to get help. That was all there was to it. With her hands and dress covered with blood, she ran as fast as she could the rest of the way up the ramp to the door of the laundry.

At first she could not get her key to open the door and she began pounding on it as she yelled for help. Just as her key finally moved the lock, someone from the inside pushed it open and almost knocked her down. By this time she was near hysteria and had to be encouraged to slow down in her speech so the laundry supervisor could understand what she was trying to say.

Then things began to happen almost too fast for Bea to comprehend. A stretcher and two strong men appeared from inside the laundry. Glenn was loaded onto it and carried post-haste to the Infirmary which was only a few yards down the tunnel. As they all trooped into the Infirmary Treatment Room, two nurses and a doctor arrived and took charge of the situation with great efficiency. An injection was given, oxygen administered, and within a few seconds, the massive convulsions began to calm. Quickly the scalp laceration was sutured and a bandage wrapped around Glenn's head. These people had obviously faced similar challenges many times before and competently fulfilled their duties in order to remedy the situation.

While all this was going on Bea stood in a corner of the Treatment Room observing and listening. Although she was shaken by the incident, the attitudes and skills she saw around her helped to calm her emotions. She had completely forgotten her laundry bag in the tunnel and the blood covering her own skin and clothing. The scarf she had carefully tied around her head before leaving her room had slid down to a position around her neck and red smeared edges dangled down over her waist and stomach. Some of the combs and clips had fallen from her head and long, loose tendrils of hair and rags hung about her face and over her shoulders.

Two attendants wheeled the sleeping Glenn to a room in the Infirmary on a gurney and one of the nurses who had assisted with the suturing turned to Bea with a sympathetic smile.

"Hi. You must be our new nurse on J-Ward," she said. "You seem to be the heroine of the week. We heard about your experiences in the barn yesterday. Have you recovered from that yet?" By the way, I'm Mrs. Anderson, this is Dr. Hector, and this is Miss Williams. Welcome to Bedlam."

Bea observed before her a tall, graceful, kind faced woman, with short, graying hair and spotless white uniform, shoes, and crisply starched cap.

The other nurse, introduced as Miss Williams, looked to be no more than sixteen or seventeen years old and her whole appearance was one of dishevelment. She was only about four and one half feet tall, with stringy, brown hair and bad teeth. She moved about in a somewhat clumsy, disjointed way, but seemed to be well oriented to the environment of the Treatment Room.

Dr. Hector was about the tallest man Bea had ever seen. She was five feet, eight inches tall herself and yet had to tip her head way back to look into his friendly, hazel eyes. He had an obvious jagged scar across the right side of his forehead and a lock of unruly red hair fell across one end of it. He looked to be about thirty years old.

The doctor greeted Bea with a friendly grin. Miss Williams offered a shy smile. Bea responded with a somewhat bashful smile and a, "How do you do?"

Both Infirmary nurses turned to begin cleaning the Treatment Room and the doctor sat down at the desk in the corner to write a note on Glenn's chart.

"You've already made quite a reputation for yourself around here," the doctor stated with a chuckle and a mischievous twinkle in his eyes. "You do seem to get yourself into messes, don't you?" he added.

It was only then that Bea was startled by her own reflection in the glass of the instrument cabinet and realized what a mess she truly was. Her face turned a flaming red to match the bloody accents on her clothes and body as she again stammered something about being glad to meet them. Then she remembered her laundry bag and murmuring something else about dirty uniforms, she rushed from the room.

Totally flustered, Bea was suddenly lost. She couldn't remember how to get back to the doorway which led down into the God forsaken tunnel. Her eyes were feeling quite moist as she stood in the middle of the infirmary hallway, not sure which way to go and too embarrassed to ask. She felt an arm go around her waist. It was Mrs. Anderson, the elder treatment room nurse.

"I was just on my way to the warehouse to get some supplies." she said. "May I walk with you to the laundry?"

Bea felt as if she had been thrown a lifeline. She gave the older nurse a weak smile and nodded silently as she allowed herself to be guided through a doorway and down the ramp toward the tunnel. As they walked along together, Mrs. Anderson talked cheerfully about some of the silly things, which the Infirmary inmates had done during breakfast that morning. By the time they arrived at the doorway to the laundry, Bea was feeling much better.

But, where was her laundry bag? There was no sign of it in the tunnel where she had dropped it. Mrs. Anderson stayed with her as they entered the laundry and introduced her to the laundry Supervisor, Mr. Grant.

He had a huge, bulbous, red nose and his clothing was soaked through with perspiration from working in the super-heated environment of the laundry. He had a strong, rancid odor about him, but seemed to be as kindly and jovial as Saint Nick himself. His whole face was bright red and his white hair was cropped close to his head. He assured Bea that he had already retrieved all her laundry and that it was being treated at that moment to remove blood stains and would be as good as new when it was returned to her on Tuesday. He handed her fresh bed and bath linens and teased her a little about being careful not to use the clean things for pillows and bandages for injured people. A side remark was also thrown in about being careful around the wrong end of mules too, and everyone within hearing laughed with gusto.

"Now, Grant, be kind to the new help." chided Mrs. Anderson, with a gentle smile. "We don't want to scare her off in the first month, do we?"

"Oh, that's all right," volunteered Bea. "I guess everyone has heard about my attempts at veterinary medicine. It is kind of funny now, but it wasn't very much fun for me when it was happening. I guess you have to learn to laugh around here to keep from crying."

"You'll do all right, Missy," replied Mr Grant. "You'll do all right."

Chapter 4

RECOVERY

————⊷⊶⊷————

M rs. Anderson accompanied Bea back to the tunnel and got her started in the right direction before they parted company. Bea talked to God all the way back to the Staff Apartment Building. She told Him that she wasn't sure she was cut out for this kind of nursing. She reasoned that she was sure she wasn't physically or emotionally strong enough to continue in this chaotic atmosphere. She asked the Lord to please show her a place to serve Him which would better suit her personal strengths and weaknesses.

But, the whole time, she kept thinking about the missionary from India, Mary Duncan, who had spoken at her church when Bea was thirteen years old. Miss Duncan had told them all about her work with patients in a leper colony near Calcutta and had shown them pictures of the horrible wounds and deformities the victims had to suffer. That presentation had been the catalyst which had influenced Bea to go into the nursing profession in the first place. Was this present assignment any worse than what Miss Duncan faced every day?

The Scripture verse from Philippians 4:13 kept running through Bea's mind.

"I can do all things through Christ which strengtheneth me."

"Oh, Lord," she cried as she walked through the dark, musty tunnel, "I know I cant do it in my own strength. If you want me to stay here, you'll have to help me every minute of every day. I just can't make it on my own."

Upon arriving back in her peaceful, orderly little apartment, Bea just wanted to collapse on her bed and sleep, but the clean linens in her arms reminded her that she still had to make her bed and take a bath before that could happen. From the blood stains on her clothes and body, it was obvious that the bath had to come first. She grabbed her bathrobe and a towel and made her way to the women's communal bathroom a few doors down the hall from her apartment. While the tub filled with hot water, she put her blood stained clothing in a sink full of cold water to soak.

Wrapping a clean towel around her disheveled locks, she stepped into the tub, sinking down until the water was up to her chin and the back of her head rested against the end of the tub. What luxury!

Her eyes closed as her thoughts returned to Mary Duncan in that Leprosarium in India. What was it that she had said about a drought there? Did Miss Duncan ever get to experience the luxury of sitting in a tub full of clean hot water, or did she have to take her baths in a contaminated stream or a small basin of water?

"Lord, bless and protect Mary Duncan," said Bea, and the next thing she knew she heard someone knocking.

Rousing from sleep, she was somewhat disoriented to find herself sitting naked in a tub full of cool water in a strange place. It took her a few seconds to realize where she was and that someone was knocking quietly on the tub room door.

"Yes?" Bea said.

"Are you all right in there?" a timid voice answered. "You've been in there a long time and I saw the bloody clothes in the sink."

"I'm so sorry," responded Bea. "I must have fallen asleep in here. Yes, I'm all right, but it has been a hectic morning. I'm getting out now and will clean the tub so you can come in."

"Oh, no," came the voice again.

"I don't want to take a bath now. I was just worried that you might be hurt."

During this exchange, Bea climbed quickly from the water, toweled dry, and slipped into her bathrobe. Opening the door, she discovered the prettiest little, blond headed girl she had ever seen, wearing a worried expression on her flawless features. Bea was struck almost speechless with the nearly angelic perfection of the girl'

"Hi," the girl said as she extended a perfectly manicured hand toward Bea. "I'm Judith. You must be Miss Jenkins. I've been hearing about you."

A mischievous smile played across her face now, and Bea was even more enchanted with her.

"Are you sure you're all right? There seems to be a lot of blood in that sink with your clothes."

Bea looked over at the sink where the clothing still lay submerged in red stained water. Suddenly the whole situation struck her funny and she began to giggle. The giggle turned into a laugh, and then into hysterical, body shaking guffaws. It was an infectious kind of laughter and before long Judith had joined in, though she had no idea what was so funny. Bea was laughing so hard that tears ran down her cheeks and she had to lean against the sink to keep from falling down.

A loud **BANG!** Surprised the laughter right out of her and she and Judith spun around toward the sound. The bathroom door had been swung open forcefully and a very large woman stood in the doorway, staring coldly at them with beady, green eyes, which were surrounded by mounds of white flesh that reminded Bea of a big bowl of mashed potatoes. A flaming red mane of unruly hair framed her head and shoulders. She was close to six feet tall, and seemed to be almost as wide as she was high. To look at her arms, one could understand why they were called, limbs. Her huge, pendulous breasts were poorly camouflaged under the long pink and brown striped dressing gown, and her abdomen made another ponderous lump below the drooping breasts. She had a maw of a mouth, with thin colorless lips and large, even, yellow teeth. She emitted a loud hissing sound and she whispered in a stage whisper with such force that it could have been heard for a city block.

"What in the (expletive) is going on in here?" she demanded, her glassy, green eyes boring into the two young women. "Don't you know there are people trying to sleep around here?" Then looking directly at Bea she asked, "Who in (expletive) are you, anyway?"

Bea opened her mouth to answer, but the giant female turned her back without waiting for a response and entered one of the toilet stalls, latching it behind her. From the stall came loud bathroom noises with accompanying odors. Judith was between Bea and the stall and she turned to face Bea, raising her eyebrows, wrinkling her nose and holding it between thumb and forefinger. Bea snorted and had to stuff a corner of her towel into her mouth to stifle more laughter.

Both young women started to remove the wet clothes from the sink and carry them to the now empty tub as if they had spoken to one another about it. They closed the door between them and the toilet area and quietly and quickly washed and wrung out Bea's things by hand and scoured out the tub.

34

They heard the large woman go back into the hall. Only then did Judith whisper to Bea.

"That was Mrs. Shipmann. She and her husband are night attendants on B-Ward in the Main Building. They've been here for years and think they own the place. She really has a foul mouth, hasn't she? Her husband is even worse. We do need to be more careful to keep quiet during the day though. Most of the people who live on this floor work on the hoot owl shift, from seven in the evening to seven in the morning, and sleep during the day. When you go on that shift you'll understand this better, and appreciate other's consideration when you're trying to sleep. Let's get back to your apartment and get these things hung up."

Like a couple of scared mice, they tiptoed silently down the hall to the door of Bea's room. Someone had placed a scrap of paper between the door and the frame, and Bea removed it before opening the door. They entered the apartment and placed the wet clothing in the kitchen sink before she unfolded the note and read aloud, in a quiet voice,

"Miss Jenkins,
Please go to Miss Peterson's office
as soon as possible. She called and
would like to speak with you."

Miss Pandora Peterson was the Director of Nursing who had hired Bea. Her office was in the Main Building, right next to Dr. Anderson's.

"Oh, Oh!" Judith exclaimed. "I'll hang up these things on the drying rack in the kitchen while you get dressed. You don't want to keep The Queen waiting. By the way, how in the world did you get to be such a bloody mess?

"Oh, that," responded Bea, as she began to climb into a fresh set of underwear and a soft, lavender dress. "When I

35

was going to the laundry through the tunnel this morning, I found one of the inmates in a grand mal seizure. He had split open his head when he hit the concrete floor of the tunnel and was bleeding from that wound and from his mouth. I got help for him, but not before I made quite a mess of myself."

"Who was the inmate?" Judith asked.

"It was a man named Glenn Schubert. This is the second time I've been in a mess with him."

"'Oh, no!" Judith exclaimed. "Glenn is such a nice person. He is so kind and gentle with everyone. He's especially good with animals and children. He's probably the nicest man I have ever known. It makes me angry when I think of people like him having this awful curse of epilepsy. Why would God let things like that happen? When I get to Heaven that is the first question I am going to ask. Is Glenn all right?"

"I think so," Bea responded. "He was sleeping peacefully when I left. They were admitting him to Infirmary West for observation. He'll probably be okay."

Then Bea told Judith about her experiences with Glenn and the mule, and they both had another laugh together but were careful not to be too loud.

"You sound like you don't like Miss Peterson very well," Bea added.

"I'm sorry. I don't want to influence your thinking before you have a chance to get to know her. Maybe she will be nice to you," apologized Judith, and then would not say any more about the nursing director.

However, as they both left the apartment Judith added, "Good luck."

She then ran quietly down the hall to her apartment, waving backward over her head as she ducked into her doorway.

Chapter 5

AUDIENCE WITH THE QUEEN

"Oh, great. Now what? Lord, help me." muttered Bea as she headed for the stairs.

She had noticed while dressing that the sun had come out and the storm was past. She was glad to use the outdoor route to the main building this time even though it had not been twenty-four hours yet since she had washed her hair. She had hurriedly pulled it back with a ribbon before leaving her apartment.

The sunshine was warm and a light breeze was blowing as she made her way toward the Main Building. As she walked quickly along the wet pavement, she wondered about Judith. Was she a nurse, or some other kind of worker? She had an interesting, soft accent of some kind. Where had she come from? Just what was her story? She seemed like the kind of person Bea could learn to like very much and could become a good friend.

Arriving at the Main Building, Bea found the office of Miss Peterson. She knocked timidly on the door and heard a voice call out,

"Come in."

37

Miss Peterson was of average height, but excruciatingly thin. She looked as if she could use some of Grandmother Stretch's home cooking. Her face was absolutely skeletal in appearance with a long pointed nose and chin. Her mousy brown hair was pulled straight back into a tight bun on the back of her head and her nurse's cap looked as if it had been made to cover her entire cranium, rather than just the top of it. She wore it so straight and forward that it sat across her forehead right above her almost non-existent eyebrows. She did not rise from her chair behind the desk as Bea hesitantly approached her.

"Have a seat, Miss Jenkins," ordered the older woman curtly, motioning to a chair across the desk from her.

"I have been hearing some disturbing things about you. Do you have anything to say for yourself?"

With that she sat with her hands folded before her over the papers on top of the desk and stared into Bea's face, which was quickly becoming quite flushed.

"I ... I don't know how to begin,' replied Bea, with downcast eyes. "Wh ... What have you heard?"

"Well, ... one thing that I heard was that you have been practicing medicine outside the scope of accepted nursing practice. I understand that you left the inmates on your ward to attend to the health needs of a mule yesterday, and that while you were thus occupied, several of those inmates escaped from that ward and became engaged in highly dangerous activities. Is that correct?"

'Wwwelll, you see, it was a little more complicated than that. They were not able to find a veterinarian and seemed to think that a nurse could help the bloated mule, which by the way, I did. And I don't believe it was my fault that the inmates got out. I locked the door behind me when I left the ward."

Then she quickly added, "And no one was hurt."

"Our administrator, Dr. Anderson, was very angry about his automobile," responded the Director.

"It will cost a great deal of money to repair and clean it. He's looking for someone to blame and you seem to be the most likely culprit."

Then the next item was broached.

"Miss Jenkins, I have been told that you were seen in the arms of one of the inmates during the whole fiasco. Is this true?"

Bea swallowed hard before answering. The scene next to the horse trough yesterday morning came back into her mind in vivid detail. There she was with wet hands and arms, in tears, being held in the muscular, tanned arms of Glenn Schubert —- an inmate. How could she explain a thing like that to someone who had not witnessed all that had transpired?

"I was upset by what had happened. I was scared. He was comforting me, that's all. He seems to be a good and gentle man. It really meant nothing to either of us. It was just one caring human being reaching out to comfort another in need. That was all it was, —- honest."

By this time, Bea was having a hard time blinking back the tears as she looked pleadingly at the straight-laced woman behind the desk. Silence hung between them as they both thought their own thoughts.

Finally, Miss Peterson spoke. "I understand that you may have saved Glenn's life this morning when you found him having a grand mal seizure in the tunnel. Is that right?"

"I got him help when he needed it," replied Bea.

"Was that the wrong thing for me to do, too?" she asked, pleadingly.

"No. You acted appropriately in that instance. However, you have managed to place yourself in a somewhat precarious position here. Doctor Anderson is blaming you for what happened in the barnyard yesterday, but his wife, Nurse Anderson and Dr. Hector both agree that you are a diamond in the rough and that with a little polishing you will turn out to be an asset to our team.

"I believe that you may just need more direction. You might not understand your exact role here. You may not understand that we have a very formalized system of behaviors. The doctors are always treated with great respect, as I am sure you were taught in nurse's training. They are never called by their first names, and always addressed as 'Doctor' so and so. When a doctor enters the room, everyone stands and remains standing until he is seated, no matter what they are doing.

"Nurses are always addressed as, 'Nurse' so and so or 'Miss' or 'Mrs.' so and so. They may call one another by their given name when they are off duty, but never in the presence of an inmate.

"Non-professional employees are usually addressed by their last names, with no title preceding it.

"Most of the inmates are addressed by their given name by everyone, though sometimes their full name is used.

"No intimate relationships are allowed between any caregiver and any inmate, no matter what their level of functioning.

"Maybe these rules of behavior were not made plain enough to you when you were hired. Do you have any questions about any of this?"

Bea replied passively, "No Ma'am"

"Good." continued Miss Peterson.

"What I would like for you to do, is to write a full report of your experiences here within the past two days and explain why you acted in the way that you did in each instance. You will be expected to submit this report to me by nine o'clock this coming Monday morning. We will then set up an appointment to discuss your report and I will give you

40

further instructions on future responsibilities and behavior we will be expecting from you. Do you understand?"

"Yes, Ma'am," answered Bea, humbly.

"Thank you. You may go."

Bea understood now why Judith had referred to the Nursing Director as, "The Queen," and she quickly retreated out of the office and back into the fresh air.

As she walked along the sidewalk, she thought, *How am I going to find time to write that report, go to that dinner party tonight, work all night Saturday night, go to church on Sunday morning, and work all night Sunday night?*

Her stomach growled at her in reply and it occurred to her that she had not had anything to eat since breakfast. Glancing at her lapel watch, she realized that she had less than an hour to dress for the dinner party and her hair needed immediate first aid. Maybe she should just send her regrets to the hostess by way of her cousin and take this evening to repair her hairdo and get started on that report.

"No, I won't!" she said to herself.

"I've had my nose to the grindstone for too long and I really need to get away from this crazy place and have a good meal in the company of normal, genteel people. I'll just have to figure out something for my hair and get myself ready to go."

41

Chapter 6

JUDITH'S STORY

B ea met Judith coming up from the Staff Recreation Room as she entered the building and they walked up to their apartments together. They whispered when they arrived on their floor and Judith stopped outside Bea's door to ask her how her audience with The Queen had gone. Bea invited her in and Judith perched on the couch while Bea quickly told her about the conference. Then Bea added that she had a dinner invitation and she needed to be ready to go in less than an hour.

Judith asked, "What are you planning to do with your hair?"

Bea moaned in reply saying, "I really don't know. Do you have any ideas?"

"Get dressed and give me a comb. I'll make you beautiful." answered Judith.

Bea quickly changed into her navy, princess style dress with white collar and cuffs and matching spectator pumps while Judith busied herself with neatly and efficiently making up the bed with the fresh linens Bea had collected from the laundry that morning.

Then Judith went to work on Bea's hair. She braided it into French braids and wound it up around her head like a crown. Then she ran to her own apartment to get her electric curling iron. With the iron, she created soft curls around Bea's face and ears and then topped off her creation with a small navy bow she had also retrieved from her rooms.

While Judith worked on her coiffure, Bea busied herself with manicure scissors, nail file, and buffer. Her Nursing Arts instructor, Sister Hazel, had frequently reminded the students in Bea's class that;

"Nurses **must** keep their nails short to prevent the spread of infection and the possible injury to a patient while working with them."

She said that one should hold one's arm strait out from the shoulder and observe the palmer side of the open hand with fingers outspread;

"If you can see the tips of your nails, they are too long. **CUT THEM!!!**"

As the girls worked, Bea began trying to get to know Judith better and to answer some of the questions she had asked herself about Judith earlier.

"Judith, where did you get that lovely accent?"
"I grew up in the State of Virginia."
"How did you come to move up here to Minnesota?"
"That's a long story, but I'll make it as short as I can.

When I was six weeks old my parents were taking me on a train to a small town in Virginia where my father had accepted a position as pastor of a new Methodist Church. The train derailed and both my parents were killed. I received a head injury and was kept in a hospital until I was transferred to a Catholic orphanage where I was baptized and raised. They couldn't find anyone who wanted to adopt me since the head injury left me with occasional convulsions, so I grew up there.

"About a year ago, I read an article in a newspaper about the Crystal Colony for epileptics in Minnesota. I decided to try my wings and applied for a job here to help take care of epileptic babies. I figured that the people here would be kind and understanding with me when I have convulsions myself. I had excellent references from the nuns and priests who knew me. I had been helping to tend babies in the orphanage since I was a little girl. They hired me here right away when they received my letter. I work on the hoot owl shift caring for the little ones and I truly love it. I believe that God has called me to this work to share His love with them."

With tears sparkling in her long lashes, she said,

"When I left the orphanage, the nuns threw a party for me. They had sold some of their prize roses in order to buy me this electric curling iron for a going away gift. It was such a sweet and thoughtful gift from them since none of them are allowed to have much hair under those hoods of theirs. They were always so good to me. I grew up with forty-two mothers, not just one like most kids."

Standing back to admire her work, Judith stated with a flourish of the comb,

"I promised to make you beautiful, but I had a lot to work with. So, between God and me we pulled it off."

Then, with a mischievous twinkle in her eyes, she added,

"The way you look now, you could be a contender for the Queen's throne."

Bea looked into the full length mirror on the back of her bedroom door and twirling around, she chuckled.

"Oh thank you, Judith. I feel like Cinderella going to the ball and you must be my fairy godmother. Thank you so much. You are a miracle worker."

With that, she gave Judith a quick hug.

Judith bubbled out a little giggle and waltzed around the room with her blond curls bouncing, while she hummed a little tune.

"You'll be Cinderella tonight. Just be sure to get home before your coach turns into a pumpkin."

Bea glanced out the window and said,

"Oh – Oh! Here's my coach now. Alan and his clan are here."

Grabbing the white, crocheted, lace shawl Grandmother Stretch had made for her, her white gloves, and a small beaded bag, she ran into the hall and down the stairs to meet her cousin.

Chapter 7

THE DINNER PARTY

———

Alan stood in the front hall of the Staff Apartment Building, strait as a soldier standing at attention, his black fedora in his hand, waiting for his cousin to make her appearance. His solemn expression was transformed into a broad smile as she came through the door from the stairs

"How handsome you are, Dear Cousin, she said, making a little curtsy to him."

"Not so much as you, my beautiful Beatrice," he answered, going along with her mock courtliness with a low bow and bringing her fingers to his lips.

Bea had always been a great admirer of her older cousin. He resembled his mother's side of the family. His maternal grandmother was a full-blooded Sioux Indian and he looked the part, with his piercing black eyes, strait jet black hair, high forehead, strong jaw, and muscular frame. This evening he wore a gray, pinstriped suit with matching spats over shiny black boots, and a starched white shirt with a celluloid collar and black string tie.

They made a striking couple as they descended the front stairs of the building and he handed her up into the surrey to sit beside his lovely but somewhat harried wife, Lydia.

She was busy answering four-year old Natalie's continual questions while attempting to calm the fussy, teething, seven-month-old Lena. After a quick, friendly greeting, Bea took over answering Natalie's questions and left Lydia to deal with the fretful baby.

This was not a very promising beginning to an evening with a group of intellectual adults. Bea was really wondering now if taking the children along was a good idea and she felt sure that Lydia would agree. Alan, on the other hand, looked totally unruffled as he guided the dapple gray horse through the streets of the city.

It was a balmy, late May evening with all the trees budding out in fresh green leaves and tulips and lilacs blooming in yards as they passed. Squirrels and chipmunks darted about and a great variety of birds could be seen and heard. They passed the potato warehouses near the railroad station and the sawmill near the river, giving Natalie many more questions to ask.

Upon arrival at the Wilkey's home, Bea was taken with the unusual architecture of the place. The house was made of native fieldstone, built into the side of a hill with many large windows reflecting the blue of the sky and the white, fluffy clouds. The architect who had designed it had been strongly influenced by the work of Frank Lloyd Wright, who was very popular at the time. The lawn was a sweeping expanse of green grass and a meandering creek spanned by an oriental style bridge could be seen at the side of the property. A great variety of lovely flower beds were scattered about in a somewhat haphazard arrangement.

Alan tied the horse to the ornate hitching post in front of the house and placed a feedbag over her head so she could have a snack while they were inside. A friendly, long legged, tan dog, with thick kinky fur, barked and jumped around him. Alan patted his head saying,

"Well, hello there, Napoleon. How are you this fine evening?"

The cousins were greeted at the door by a vision of loveliness, in the person of Inga Thorson. She was a distant relative of Mrs. Wilkey. Inga was a bond servant from Sweden. The Wilkey's had sponsored her to come to this country to work for them as a maid for seven years. In return for her services, she was given traveling money from Sweden, room and board in their home, college tuition, tutoring in English, and a small stipend for personal needs. She was a large boned, well rounded girl with twinkling eyes, naturally pink cheeks, and a scattering of freckles across the bridge of her nose, like happy children playing on a cream colored hill. A thick blond braid hung down the middle of her back to her waist, tied at the end with a sky blue ribbon, matching her dress and eyes. A crisp, white apron finished off her costume. She instantly enchanted the guests with her infectious smile and charming accent.

"Welcome. Please come in," she said in broken English, as she took Alan's hat and immediately began cooing over the children.

Mrs. Wilkey appeared behind her and gently, but firmly, reminded her that she should see to her duties in the kitchen. Inga blushed and placing Alan's hat on the hall coat rack, she smiled demurely, curtsied, and hurried away.

The guests were escorted into the dining room, followed quietly by Napoleon. Professor Wilkey and the other guests were already gathered around a large, glass topped, oval table. The whole home appeared to be very modern, with Danish Modern furniture and Art Nuevo lamps and other accessories. Arrangements of fresh, colorful, wild and cultured flowers abounded everywhere. The overall effect of the home impressed Bea as if she had stepped into a beautiful fantasy.

The men at the table rose as Mrs. Wilkey made introductions. Bea and her cousins were seated at the table with Alan beside the Professor, Lydia next to him with Lena on her lap, and Natalie perched atop a thick dictionary between Lydia and Bea. The rest of the party was made up of professional people including the new Lutheran minister, Rev. Larson, and his wife and their towheaded son, Timmy, sitting on a thick tome between them. Dr. and Mrs. Anderson and Dr. Hector completed the guests.

Everyone greeted the newcomers graciously except for Professor Wilkey, who paused only briefly and nodded toward them as he continued to expounded on the Greco-Roman Wars in a monotone voice. Napoleon lay sprawled on the oriental carpet beside his master's chair with his head resting on his outstretched front legs and his eyes staring straight ahead as if mesmerized by the sound of the professor's monologue.

Bea found herself sitting across the table from Dr. Hector who met her eyes with a warm, friendly smile. For some reason she felt embarrassed by his gaze, remembering how he had last seen her, covered with blood and rags hanging from her hair. She was glad that Natalie took up so much of her attention so she did not feel the need to look in his direction often.

The meal commenced quickly after the pastor had returned grace. Inga had obviously been well trained in serving. Everything went along without a hitch. The table had been set with clear glass and crystal dishes and stemware. The silver flatware and candlesticks had been polished to a warm glow which reflected the light of the slender, white tapers and irises gracing the centerpiece.

The menu consisted of Du Barry Soup, followed with Garcia Salad, Steak A' la Victor Hugo, Creamed Asparagus tips, Potato croquettes, and Parker House Rolls with fresh creamery butter and raspberry preserves making up the main course. Bread and butter pickles graced a fanciful, flower petal shaped bowl. Lemonade and Elderberry wine were served, as well as chilled milk for the children. Dessert was a specialty of Inga's: Swedish Rice Pudding, made from her own mother's recipe.

Everyone seemed to be enjoying the food, but conversation between them was very limited since the honorable professor managed somehow to continue unabated with his boring diatribe on ancient history. He seemed not to hear any other conversation, nor to notice any other activities in the room as he droned on and on.

Bea was kept pretty busy between eating her own meal and helping Natalie cut up her meat and choose which piece of flat ware for each item on her plate. However she was seated in a spot that gave her a clear view of Professor and Mrs. Wilkey and the dog, Napoleon. At the beginning of the meal, she started to wonder how the professor could manage to talk without missing a beat while at the same time eating his meal. It took her some time to figure out how the food on his plate kept disappearing as he did not have his mouth full while he spoke.

Suddenly she noticed what was actually happening.

The professor watched his wife at the other end of the table the whole time and when she glanced away from him, his hand snatched some food from his plate and quick as a wink it was in Napoleon's mouth. The dog didn't move a muscle, didn't even bat an eyelid during this maneuver. It happened so fast and innocuously that no one else at the table seemed to notice it was happening. Then, as Bea observed Mrs. Wilkey, she noticed that every once in a while, the hostess had a small, fleeting frown in conjunction with the secretive shenanigans taking place at the other end of the table, but not one word was said about it.

The rice pudding was a favorite of the two older children and occasionally, between bites they giggled at one another across the table. Lena had gone to sleep on Lydia's lap almost as soon as she was exposed to the monotonous voice at the head of the table, thus relieving the guests of the irritation of a fussy baby and giving her mother at least one free hand to enjoy the meal.

All the guests at the table appeared to relish the food. Complements came often. Some of the ladies even asked for recipes.

Natalie had finished eating her second helping of pudding when she tugged on on her mother's sleeve whispering,

"Mommy, I need to use the potty."

Inga, standing nearby, interjected quietly.

"I will take her," and quickly the two disappeared in the direction of the kitchen.

The other guests, with their stomachs full, were beginning to have trouble keeping their eyes from closing. As a matter of fact, Dr. Anderson, his plump chin resting on his palm and elbow propped on the table beside his pudding bowl, was heard emitting soft snoring sounds. His wife did not even attempt to disturb him. She might have been envying him a little herself.

Suddenly a horrified scream was heard emitting from the direction of the kitchen, followed by excited feminine verbalizations in a foreign tongue. Everyone at the table jumped. Even Doctor Anderson was roused from his reverie with his scalp moving violently back and forth. Professor Wilkey frowned slightly and skipped a beat in his ongoing story.

Mrs. Wilkey quickly rose and, with a quick, "Excuse me." exited toward the sounds in the kitchen. She was followed by the barking, Napoleon. The sleeping Lena immediately awoke and set up a wail, and very shortly thereafter the "trip-trip-trip" of the childish running footsteps of Natalie was heard coming from the same direction. As she arrived back in the dining room. She threw herself onto her mother in tears which made Lena howl even louder. Professor Wilkey finally stopped talking and with a bewildered expression rose from the table and stood gazing toward the door. Alan and Bea exchanged worried glances as Lydia attempted to calm the two children. Across the table, Timmy was bouncing up and down in excitement.

Then they all heard Mrs. Wilkey call,

"Come everyone. Come and see something wonderful."

The group needed no second invitation, as they were all overcome with curiosity by this time. They quickly trooped into the kitchen to find the maid and her mistress gazing at the north wall of that room where Mrs. Wilkey had been creating a mural. The wall was painted flat white and upon that canvas of white had been painted numerous geometric shapes in many different sizes and colors. The mural was not yet completed and paint and brushes had been left on a small table beside the work.

Gesturing toward Natalie, the hostess said,

"She said it was a map," and then waved her hand toward black, curving lines between the colored geometric shapes on the lower portion of the mural.

"I love it!" she chortled.

"Who wants to name the cities?" she continued.

"I'll name the first one."

Picking up a small paintbrush, and dipping it into the black paint, she printed, **MADISON** beside a medium sized, bright orange trapezoid.

"Come on." she insisted.

"There's enough brushes and paint for everyone."

At first, they all just stared at her in disbelief, but then Dr. Hector and Mrs. Anderson each picked up brushes and, with grins on their faces began labeling the colored shapes.

"Can I draw roads, too?" squealed Timmy. His father shrugged his shoulders and handed him a brush, while pulling a chair up to the wall for him to stand upon.

"You too, Natalie," Mrs. Wilkey said, as she pulled a stool up next to the wall.

"You gave us the idea. Help us finish this map."

Natalie's tears had disappeared as if by magic as she looked questioningly at her parents. Her mother was still too much involved in trying to calm the crying baby to answer her, but her father gave her a grave nod and she climbed up onto the proffered stool and began drawing in roads.

Lydia retreated to a bedroom to nurse Lena and the kitchen was filled with laughter filled joking. Even Dr. Anderson and Professor Wilkey got into the act.

The map turned out to be a total fantasy with everyone printing in the name of his or her own favorite cities. **PARIS** was connected to **COPENHAGEN**, which was connected to **CAMBRIDGE**. **ATLANTA** was just down the road from **DENVER** and **SAINT PAUL** was a neighbor to **LISBON**. The host even had a chance to get **ROME** and **ATHENS** on the map.

When roads had connected all the shapes and each of them had a name, they all stood back and inspected their work as they laughed together. Collars had been unbuttoned, ties loosened, shawls discarded and hairpins dropped. Paint spots besmirched Sunday clothes, but everyone wore a smile and as they took their departure they were all filled with good food and a jolly feeling of friendship and good will.

Everything was quiet when they arrived back at the colony and they said hurried good nights. Bea used her key to let herself in and tiptoed to her apartment. She thought briefly about the report that had to be written before Monday as she undressed and brushed her hair one hundred stokes as her grandmother had taught her. Her eyelids drooped, but she opened her Bible before turning out the light and read from Romans 8:28,

> ***"...All things work together for good to those who love God, to them who are called according to His purpose."***

"Thank You, Lord, for helping us through another difficult situation and thank you for giving your children a sense of humor," she said with a smile as she climbed into bed.

Chapter 8

STORMS OF MIND AND SKY

Saturday dawned foggy and misty. Bea didn't even stir from her bed until almost ten o'clock. She slept as only the young, innocent, or dead can; peacefully and without worry or guilt. The cares of the world are still there, but this kind of slumber blocks them all out so that none of it is important.

When she did finally rise, she looked into the bathroom mirror and realized that her hair had to be her top priority again. It was a mountain of frizz from the braiding she had brushed out the night before and it needed to be brought under control. She wet it all down and then repeated the whole waving and curling routine with clips, combs, and rags.

While reading from the Psalms, she heard a gentle tap on her door. Still wearing her dressing gown, she opened it a crack and found Judith outside in the hall.

"Come in," she said with a smile as she swung the door open wide and her new friend bounced inside.

"I thought you would never wake up," Judith began with no preamble.

"How did the party go? What was their house like? What did they give you to eat? What was everyone wearing? Is Professor Wilkey as boring as everyone says?"

One question tumbled out after another with hardly a breath in between.

"Wait a minute, one question at a time I didn't know you could talk so fast with that southern accent," answered Bea laughingly.

"Have a seat and I'll make us some coffee while we talk. I can't believe I could be so hungry again after all the food we ate last night, but I am. What time is it anyway?"

She looked around for her lapel watch which she had taken off the afternoon before.

"It's after ten and I've been up all night working and couldn't go to sleep this morning. I was waiting for you to wake up so I could hear about the dinner. Since I didn't get to go, the least you can do is tell me about it," Judith answered with a mock pout.

Bea grinned at her and told her the entire story of the previous night's adventures as she prepared and served coffee and toast from her kitchenette. When she came to the part about the wall mural "map," they both had to stifle peals of laughter in their sleeves to keep from making enough noise to wake the other residents of the building.

When the narrative of the previous evening's events came to an end, Judith asked another question.

"What do you think of Dr. Hector? I think he's just the cat's pajamas."

Bea's cheeks flamed and it was obvious that the comment had flustered her.

"He's nice — but he's soooo tall," She answered.

"Last night he was the only one there who could reach all the way to the top of that map without standing on something."

This sent Judith into another fit of laughter, and she buried her face in her arms and shook so hard that Bea was afraid that she was going into an epileptic convulsion.

With a look of alarm she asked,

"Judith, are you all right?"

Judith shook her head in the affirmative as she continued to giggle into her arms. Then jumping up from the chair, she began dancing about the room, arms lifted high, looking up toward the ceiling and humming a lively tune as if she were dancing with a very tall partner. She danced into the bedroom where she collapsed on the bed burying her face in the pillow as she continued to laugh.

Suddenly Judith emitted a shrill cry like the warning call of a peacock and her body stiffened and began to jerk all over in a true grand mal seizure. Bea followed her into the bedroom attempting to contain her own merriment to an acceptable level and saw the change occur. She immediately recognized the difference in Judith's body and knew that she had a true seizure to contend with now. She rolled Judith onto her side and made sure that her airway was clear. Moving swiftly to the kitchenette, she grabbed a teaspoon and a dishcloth. Wrapping the cloth around the spoon, she gently wedged it between the girl's teeth and watched carefully as the shaking continued for three or four minutes.

Slowly, Judith's respirations became quieter and her body began to relax. Her eyes regained their focus as she looked up at Bea and dropped the cloth wrapped spoon from her mouth.

She asked in a soft, slightly slurred voice,

"Was it a bad one?"

"It was hard, but only lasted three or four minutes and you seem to be alright." answered the young nurse with tears in her eyes.

"You are just too tired and excited. I'm going to sit here at the desk and begin to write my report for the Queen. You just turn over and go to sleep and I'll watch to make sure you're alright. Okay?"

There was no argument as Judith turned away from Bea and promptly began to snore softly in a deep sleep. Bea had learned that this was typical following a seizure of this type.

"Lord, help her and help me to be a good friend to her," Bea prayed silently as she moved carefully about gathering paper and pen to begin writing her report, with buttered toast and coffee at her elbow.

At first, the report seemed too great a task to accomplish. How could she tell the whole story in such a way that Miss Peterson and Dr. Anderson would understand how and why she had acted as she had and find it in their hearts to give her another chance to prove herself as a responsible nurse?

Then she was reminded of Professor Kuski, her Microbiology instructor. He had taught her to examine each experiment from every possible point of view, record every detail exactly as observed, consider every possible reason for the outcome, and record it all in concise language. She would have to approach this situation as if it were one of her Microbiology experiments and write it up in the same manner. She realized that this would be an enormous labor and time intensive way to approach the problem, but that it would probably go a long way toward gaining faith and respect from her superiors. So that is the way she began.

The noon hour came and went with no further thought of food, and Judith continued to slumber in Bea's bed, as she filled page after page with her neat, manuscript writing. Occasionally, she would crumple up a page and reach for a fresh one to make sure that there were no errors in spelling, grammar, punctuation or facts.

Throughout the afternoon, Judith continued in her deep sleep and Bea was constantly aware of her even breathing.

Bea was only vaguely aware that changes were taking place outside the windows. The sky had blackened. Rain was falling heavily against the panes. Occasional flashes of lightning reflected on the wall opposite the bedroom window and loud thunderclaps shook the building. As she continued to write, hailstones began to strike the windows.

Then, everything grew silent as if someone had turned off the tap of a faucet. This silence finally drew Bea's attention to the scene outside and as she rose to look through the window, she heard a new sound. It sounded to her as if a distant freight train was heading toward the building. She saw through the window a funnel cloud, swirling straight toward her and she knew that she had to move quickly.

She screamed Judith's name as she attempted to shake her awake.

"Judith! Judith, wake up! There's a tornado headed straight this way! We've got to get to the tunnel fast!"

Jerking the groggy girl to a standing position, she all but carried her out of the apartment and down the hallway toward the stairs as she sounded a loud yelling alarm to the other occupants of the floor.

"Get to the tunnel, fast! There's a tornado coming!"

She hollered in the voice she used to use to call the farm hands in from the fields when she was a girl living on her grandparents' farm.

As she dragged Judith down the hall, she paused long enough at each apartment door to pound on it three times with her fist and continued to raise the alarm. Coming to the stairwell door, she grabbed the handle on the fire alarm and as that clamor began she plunged down the stair, half dragging, half carrying Judith along with her.

The roar around her was deafening as they ducked through the doorway into the tunnel. Once safely inside, she released her hold on her friend, who slid slowly down the concrete block wall to the where she sat, dazed and staring up at Bea in frank bewilderment.

Other residents of the building were piling quickly through the tunnel door in various states of undress and dishevelment. Everyone was talking at once, and the tunnel echoed with their panicked voices, the clanging of the fire alarm, and the roar of the storm above. Then the fire alarm was cut off in mid clang. The lights in the tunnel were extinguished and everyone became quiet including the giantess, Mrs. Shipman, who stood in a long, tomato worm green and orange print nightgown caught in mid-curse with her mouth hanging open.

The sound of the storm continued unabated for several minute and the tunnel floor trembled under their feet. Some of the women were crying quietly. Some were clinging to their husbands or one another.

Then came the silence. Only the sound of raindrops could be heard on the skylights overhead. Everything else was still.

A loud, commanding, masculine voice came out of the darkness preceded by several spicy, swear words. He said, "I think it's over. I'll go see," and he cautiously attempted to open the door of the tunnel leading back into the apartment building, but the door wouldn't budge.

Two other men tried to help him but found that they could not open the door either. A little more light was coming through the sky lights by then.

"We need to go to the next building and try to get out," came the same commanding voice.

"I've been in this (expletive) tunnel in the middle of the night when the lights went out and it's really dark then. Here's what we need to do. Listen up! Find the person next to you and put your right hand on their right shoulder. Then feel the wall with your left hand. We're going to head for Building Five. If we can't get in there, we'll just go on along this (expletive) tunnel 'till we get to an (expletive) door that'll open. That storm couldn't have taken out all eight buildings in this colony."

It was then that Bea started to feel the fear that she had not taken time to notice until now.

What if we are buried alive in this tunnel? She thought. *How will we get out?*

By this time Judith had regained enough wakefulness to have found strength to stand.

"That's Mr. Shipman," she whispered.

Without another word, Bea placed her hand on the right shoulder of the woman on her right. She felt Judith's hand on her own shoulder, and they followed the others down the tunnel, trailing their left hands along the clammy, concrete block wall.

Mr. Shipman led the way to the first door which led into Cottage five. A key was produced and the door unlocked and opened without any trouble. A unison sigh of relief could be heard as the group crowded through the doorway, and they began to talk excitedly among themselves again.

As they hurried up the concrete ramp into the basement of Cottage Five, they noticed that the ramp floor was slippery and wet. The sound of agitated talking, screaming and crying came from above. Toping the ramp, they turned to view the dining room of the building. The lower functioning inmates were still tethered to the wall at the dining room tables, not having finished eating their noon meal when the storm hit. The higher level ones were running about, talking excitedly, crying, or pacing. The attendants had clearly lost control of the situation. Water was coming through broken windows on the west side of the room.

As if they had all practiced this kind of disaster before, the partially clad attendants and nurses from the tunnel calmly pitched in to help. Mr. Shipman took command of the situation again and began assigning work details. This little man stood in the dining room, bandy legged, in his long, white "Union Suit" and white cotton socks, his sparse, gray hair standing on end, yelling commands like an Army Sergeant.

Actually, it was easy for him to take on this role, since he had been a Sergeant in the Army Medical Corps in India during the Great World War. He sent some of the staff to assess the damage on the upper floor of the building. Two men were sent to the Main Building to report to the administration. The nurses began checking people for injuries. A clean up crew was assigned.

The lower functioning and upset inmates were taken to a dry, quiet exercise room on the east side of the basement where everyone was encouraged to rest on the tumbling mats on the floor. There Judith began singing happy little nursery rhyme songs with them, like: "Hey Diddle Diddle, the Cat and the Fiddle," "Old MacDonald Had A Farm, and "Twinkle, Twinkle, Little Star." She seemed to be back to her usual, effervescent, cheerful self. Within a few minutes a semblance of order was regained as everyone worked together to try to make things as normal as possible once again.

As Bea worked beside the other professionals, non-professionals, and higher level inmates, the thought occurred to her that all the rules of separation of classes had flown away with the storm. Everyone was working together to reach a common goal without thought of whose job it was or who was more important than anyone else. She wanted to tell Miss Peterson that this is the way things should always be, but she felt that old ways would quickly come back into play as soon as things settled down.

The men who had been sent to the Main Building returned, accompanied by Dr. Anderson and Miss Peterson.

They reported that the Staff Apartment Building had been totally destroyed and that the upper floor of the building they were in now had been badly damaged. They said that these two buildings were the only ones which had sustained serious damage. Other than several broken windows, many fallen tree limbs, a scattered haystack, and some frightened livestock, there didn't seem to be any other damage. The administrative staff had been busy attempting to account for the safety of all the inmates, staff, and visitors who were known to be at the colony that day.

Although everyone on the staff was required to live at the colony, most of the day staff workers were either at work in another building, shopping in town, or visiting friends or relatives in the surrounding community when the storm hit. The children of staff members were not allowed to live at the colony with their parents. They were boarded out with family or friends, and their parents went to see them on their days off.

All of the doctors lived in private bungalows around the edges of the colony except Dr. and Mrs. Anderson, whose home was directly across the street from the Main Building in the center of the colony.

By this time everyone had been accounted for, and they were told that if the inmates of Building Five had not been in the basement and the staff had not been so quick getting out of their apartments, there would probably have been many casualties and possible fatalities.

Mrs. Shipman swiveled around to look toward Bea when she heard that.

"It was the new girl." she said.

"We were all asleep and she woke us up."

Striding over to Bea, she grabbed her shoulders and looking directly into her eyes she softly said, "Your loud mouth saved our lives."

Then she enveloped Bea with those beefy arms and gave her a huge bear hug.

When Bea came up for air, she looked around and saw many expressions of gratitude on the faces of the staff members who had been sleeping in their apartments before the tornado hit. They surrounded her and patted her on the back; a rag-tag group in a variety of sleepwear, some with bare feet, and all with rumpled hair.

Suddenly, Bea felt totally exhausted, and she began to sob uncontrollably. Comforting arms and words upheld her as she saw the world spinning around her, and she slumped into unconsciousness.

When she aroused from her stupor, Bea looked up to see her cousin, Alan bending over her.

He asked, "Are you feeling better now?"

Miss Peterson was looking over his shoulder and asked, "Do you feel well enough to go with your cousin to his home to get some rest? You've earned an extra day off from work. Try to get some sleep and if you feel well enough you can begin your training on the night shift tomorrow night —alright?"

Bea nodded her head in mute assent as Alan and Mrs. Shipman helped her to her feet. She leaned heavily on them as they started up the stairs to the front door.

What should I be taking care of? What have I forgotten? She was thinking as she started from the building.

Suddenly it came to her. Turning around with eyes wide, she moaned.

"Miss Peterson, the wind blew my report away. It was almost finished. It's gone!"

With that she began to weep again in great, hiccuping sobs.

The Director came swiftly to her side and said, in soothing tones,

"Don't worry about that report now. We'll think and talk about it later."

Then glancing around at the disarray, she added,

"Much later, I think."

"Oh, thank you," Bea gulped.

"Thank you so much."

Then Alan and her new friend, Mrs. Shipman, assisted her down the littered front steps to the waiting carriage where she was wrapped with a buffalo robe. She didn't notice the sun now peeping from between tattered clouds, nor the rainbow between the trees of the apple orchard. Her eyes were closed and as the mare clip-clopped along in an easy rhythmic trot she snuggled down on the leather seat and slept.

Chapter 9

A PLACE TO REST

⸺⟊⟊⟊⸺

Alan and Lydia's home was cozy, but small. It only had two bedrooms, so Bea was tucked into the master bedroom to sleep with Natalie's calico cat, Samantha, curled up, purring on the foot of the bed. At first Bea slept soundly, but then she was awakened by Lena's screams as she suffered with the pain of teething. A pillow over Bea's head only stifled the sounds minimally and she soon gave up and made an appearance in the kitchen where a harried, Lydia was trying to calm the baby.

Lydia apologized for the noise and seemed to be at her wit's end to try to figure out how to adapt her home to the addition of another adult. She poured cups of coffee for Bea and herself and then sat at the table with her, while holding Lena on her lap, rocking back and forth and rubbing the baby's gums with her finger. Lena calmed to a soft, occasional whimper. Bea sipped the coffee, feeling lost and in the way. The rags, combs and clips in her hair were all a'kilter. She still wore her bedroom slippers and her nightgown under her dressing gown. Her face was puffy from tears and sleep and she hid a yawn behind her hand. She was never so tempted to return to Grandmother Stretch's home as she was right then.

As they sat there, each absorbed in her own thoughts trying to figure out what to do, a light tapping was heard at the back door. Lydia called out, "Come in," and Lena began to squall again.

The door opened and the cheery face of Inga, the Wilkey's maid, appeared. Her message was simple. Mrs. Wilkey had heard of the storm damage at the Crystal Colony and had sent Inga to fetch Bea to stay with them, knowing that there really wasn't room for a guest to sleep at Alan and Lydia's house.

"The Lord does take care of His own," Bea exclaimed as she thanked Lydia for her willingness to try to help her. Wrapping a quilt around her, she followed Inga out to the buggy parked behind the house.

"I must look like a real ragamuffin to anyone who sees me today," she commented as they drove toward the Wilkey residence.

"I feel like this day is never going to end."

These comments seemed to tickle Inga. She had never heard of a ragamuffin before and the term seemed comical to her. She exploded in laughter and every time she seemed to be starting to control herself, she would erupt with it again. Her sounds of glee were infectious to Bea, and soon she found herself joining in the joviality. Inga would look at Bea and say in her heavily accented English,

"You look like a real raggy-muffin."

Then they would burst out in rollicking laughter all over again.

Upon arrival at the Wilkey house, the carriage was met by Napoleon, wagging his stub of a docked tail so hard that his whole hind quarters gyrated back and forth in time with his happy welcoming barks. He immediately adopted Bea and followed close behind her every move. In the kitchen, Inga made Bea some chamomile tea. While drinking it, Bea's eyelids began to droop. Inga tucked her into the tastefully decorated guest room, pulling the drapes to keep out the sunlight, which had returned in full brilliance.

Bea was asleep almost as quickly as her head nestled into the goose down filled, satin covered pillow. Her last thought before succumbing to sleep was, *Thank you, Lord for keeping us all safe, but is this what you call, "Leading me beside the still waters?"*

She awoke early on Sunday morning to the songs of the cardinals perched in the blue spruce outside the window.

"Praise the Lord!" she said aloud.

"God is still in His Heaven, and all is right with the world." With that she turned over and went back to sleep.

Supper was served before Professor Wilkey drove Bea to work. Inga ate with them at the small, round, maple table in the kitchen. Bea noticed that Napoleon did not get much from the table that evening. Professor Wilkey evidently favored the menu of this meal above the one for the dinner party on Friday. Fried chicken, mashed potatoes, milk gravy, green beans, fresh baked biscuits, dandelion green salad, and apple pie made up this meal.

The professor was exceptionally quiet as Bea related to them, from her perspective the story of the tornado of the day before. Of course, after she had exhausted that subject, he had to top it with the story of the destruction of Pompeii by the eruption of Mount Vesuvius in seventy-nine A.D. He explained that his father, the archaeologist, had worked for several years on the excavation of the ruins of Pompeii. He also said that he and his mother had spent five summers there with his father.

No wonder he's so obsessed with ancient history, thought Bea.

When supper had ended, Mrs. Wilkey took Bea on a tour of the home, reminding her that she should feel free to make herself at home there for as long as she wanted to stay.

The room which took Bea's breath away more than any other, was the library. A huge fireplace dominated one wall. All the furniture was large, chintz covered, and comfortable looking. Windows covered the whole west wall, looking out over the grassy lawn, flowers, and creek. Bird feeders hung from the overhang. But the best part of the room was the books. Book shelves covered two walls from ceiling to floor. It seemed to Bea to be an absolute treasure trove of books. Although many of the volumes were on art, archeology, and history, there were also many other subjects included. She quickly discovered that they included the full collection of Jean Stratton-Porter's writings. She was ecstatic to discover this, since she had been mourning the loss of her new book, which she had not had time to read before it had been destroyed by the storm. She was also pleased to find a large family Bible on a reading stand and felt a pang of loss for her own Bible, which had been given to her for ten years of perfect attendance in Sunday School.

Chapter 10

THE HOOT OWL SHIFT

—ᴇᴠ—

Bea arrived at the Area Nurse's Office at six o'clock, on Sunday night. She was an hour early for her first training night on the hoot owl shift. She felt totally refreshed after sleeping through Saturday night and most of Sunday. She felt bad about missing church this morning, but had been encouraged by Inga and Mrs. Wilkey to get plenty of rest before beginning work all night.

Fresh uniforms had been delivered to the Wilkey home from the colony's laundry and many nice clothes and shoes had arrived for her from various homes and businesses in the community. Word of her acts of heroism had spread quickly throughout the town of River Ridge and many people wanted to help reward her for this. Erickson's Jewelers had even sent her a beautiful, new, silver lapel watch.

She was greeted warmly in the Infirmary Area Nurse's office by Miss Humphrey, the full time night shift Area Nurse and the Nursing Director, Miss Peterson who was considered the Area Nurse of the day shift when she was on duty.

"My goodness, you're early! That's good!" exclaimed Miss Humphrey, with a toothy smile.

The word, "toothy" was almost an understatement. She had a mouthful of huge, brilliantly white, protruding teeth, the likes of which Bea had never before seen. It was difficult to keep from staring at them as she continued.

"I can always tell what kind of worker a person will be by promptness. You just earned a few points in my book."

Again, she favored Bea with her jack-0-lantern smile.

After introductions, Bea explained to the two that her nurse's caps had been blown away in the storm and Miss Peterson gave her permission to go bare headed until new ones could be obtained.

They began Bea's orientation to the Night Shift Area Nurse position by telling her a little about what would be expected of her. They explained that Miss Humphrey worked six nights in a row every week, with Saturday nights off. On her regular nights off and during her vacation and holiday time, the other nurses in the Colony took turns replacing her.

"Of course, no one can really replace Miss Humphrey," added Miss Peterson earnestly. "No one else knows the routine or the night staff as well as she does. But the Professional Nurses do their best to try to relieve her for her time off. By the way, Mrs. Anderson takes my place as Area Nurse when I am off duty during the day."

The two older nurses then went on to explain that there were only four trained nurses on duty during the night shift, the Area Nurse and three nurses in the infirmary. The Area Nurse made rounds to all the wards every two hours and was on call for any emergency and to answer any nursing care questions, which the direct care attendants might have during the night. If a doctor was needed, the Area Nurse was the one who called the doctor who was "on call." The physicians took turns for this duty.

The Area Nurse was also the one who took care of any emergency with the buildings or grounds during the night, and she had a list of people to call for anything she could not handle on her own. This list included all the doctors, nurses, pharmacists, and attendants, as well as the supervisors of the laundry, maintenance, and farm. Other people on this list included people from the surrounding community; the sheriff, fire department, mortician, dentist, and pastors of all the churches.

Miss Humphrey said that this list was her life line and that she wouldn't even try to do her job without these people to call on in an emergency, though she admitted to having used a wrench and giving some first aid and spiritual counseling herself many times.

"We try to be pretty self sufficient most of the time," she added. "Most people don't take kindly to be awakened in the middle of the night, so we try to patch up whatever or whomever is in need of help until the day timers get their eyes open and their brains turned back on."

At this point, Miss Peterson gave a brief, concise report of all new and unusual happenings on the day shift. Following this she said, while removing her cap,

"Well, I'll leave you to the tender mercies of Miss Humphrey now, Miss Jenkins. Have a good night. I will see you in the morning."

With a nod and brief smile, she moved smoothly from behind the desk and left the two alone.

It was then that Bea realized that the Nursing Director moved from place to place as if she were floating. It was almost wraith like. For some reason Bea felt a brief chill go through her body and felt the fine hairs on the back of her neck stand up on end.

I hope I don't ever come upon her unexpectedly in the tunnel, she thought to herself.

"Well," said Miss Humphrey, "it's time for us to introduce you to the staff and inmates and the night routine. We'll make our Eight o'clock rounds now and then I'll show you how to do some of the paper work you'll be responsible for.

With that Bea followed Miss Humphrey down the Infirmary hallway toward the East Wing. Upon entering the Infirmary East-Ward, the first thing Bea heard was the soft, musical southern voice of her new friend, Judith, who was talking quietly to the diminutive, grossly deformed face of a dark skinned boy she held in her arms. His eyes were glued to her face as she spoke. Bea felt a warm glow and tears filled her own eyes at the picture of the angelic looking girl sharing unconditional love with a child most people would be repulsed by. His twisted body and monstrous features only accented the depth of her devotion and benevolence. She didn't even notice the two nurses as they stood watching her and she only looked up with a brilliant smile when Miss Humphrey spoke her name.

When asked where she was staying now, she replied that the Benedictine Sisters at a nearby convent had taken her in until a new staff apartment building could be built. She said that they were very nice to her and she was comfortable with them. They even furnished transportation for her to go forth and back to work.

Bea was introduced to the other attendants and the nurse in charge, as she and Miss Humphrey quietly made the rounds of the cribs and one full sized bed in the unit.

"This ward is reserved for babies and other small inmates who are too fragile to live out in the other buildings," explained Mrs. Brown, who was the nurse in charge. "They're all like delicate china dolls that need very gentle and constant care and attention. We are pretty protective of them." As she was speaking, she led the way over to a corner where an inmate lay on a full sized bed.

"This is Joy," she said, with a smile.

Bea was amazed as she looked at the figure lying before her. The smiling face she saw was in the center of a huge head, which spread across the entire width of the bed on which it lay. The skin covering her head was stretched so far that her soft, fine, flaxen hair was sparsely scattered over her pink scalp. Her small pearly teeth lay in straight rows as she favored the nurses with a brilliant smile. Her cornflower blue eyes moved from one nurse to the other, bright with interest and anticipation. The caregivers had dressed her diminutive body in a pink ruffled nightgown. Miss Humphrey held her delicate hand in hers as she introduced the girl to Bea.

"Joy is our angel," she said as she stroked her arm. "She always gives us a smile, and we believe God has sent her to us to make us understand how blessed we all are. No matter how hard a day we are having, all we have to do is visit with Joy, and she makes us feel better.

"Joy, this is our new nurse, Miss Jenkins. She will be working at night some of the time when I am off duty. You're really going to like her. Isn't she pretty?"

Bea took Joy's free hand and gave it a little shake. And told her she was happy to meet her. As Joy met Bea's eyes it seemed that a soft, peaceful feeling was exchanged between the two.

Then with a soft pat on Joy's head, Mrs. Humphrey added, "Go to sleep now Angel. We'll see you in the morning."

Bea had seen pictures in her textbooks of hydrocephalic children when she was in nurse's training, but she had never seen one in person. When they had moved out of Joy's ear-shot she asked,

"How old is Joy? I was taught that children like that couldn't live very long."

"They normally don't," answered Miss Humphrey, "but she will be seventeen years old next week. It's really a mir-acle, but I believe that God has helped her nurses, attendants, and doctors to give her such good care that she has been

74

able to survive this long. She has frequent fits, kidney infections, lung infections, constipation, and sores on her head and body from lack of physical activity. She is very difficult to move from one position to another as you can imagine, but she receives excellent care here."

Bea noticed that Miss Humphrey had used the old fashion term, "fits" instead of the more recently accepted terms, "seizure," or "Convulsions," but she didn't question the Area Nurse about that.

At that point, a shrill, hawk like cry was heard from another corner of the ward, and the staff all hurried to the crib of a small boy. He was in a grand mal seizure with back arched, eyes rolled back, and his entire body thrashing about. Mrs. Brown rushed to get an injection of Phenobarbital while Judith carefully forced an adhesive tape wrapped wooden tongue blade between the boy's teeth and packed pillows around his body to keep him from injuring hie limbs. The sides of his crib were already padded for this purpose.

As the boy continued to writhe, Miss Humphrey explained to Bea that this was Stevie. At the age of ten months, he had been left playing in the tub on a hot day and had been found face down in the water. His mother had been able to revive his breathing by turning him upside down and hitting him on the back, but his brain had already been damaged, and now he had many fits each day. He was now four years old, but his body had not grown since the accident.

After the Phenobarbital had been administered, Stevie's body slowly relaxed. His diaper was changed and the perspiration and drool around his mouth were gently sponged away. Clean bedding and gown were supplied. And he lay quietly with long dark lashes lying against his pale cheeks. He was truly a beautiful child.

Bea was becoming more and more depressed as she looked around her and saw the children in their cribs. Most of the cribs had padding around the inside of the side rails, and she realized that this was probably to protect them from flailing limbs and bodies like Stevie's. As she and Miss Humphrey moved from crib to crib, Bea was introduced to each inmate and a brief medical history was given as well as any current concerns.

After completing their rounds on East-Ward, the two nurses moved to the West-Ward of the Infirmary. Miss Humphrey explained that this ward was where inmates who were acutely ill or recovering from surgery or a serious injury were cared for. This meant that inmates with all levels of intelligence were mixed together on this ward. It had the most nursing staff on duty at all times than anywhere else in the colony. There were at least two graduate nurses and two other attendants on every shift.

Upon arrival in the West-Ward, the first person Bea noticed was Glenn Schubert. He was sitting in the day room smoking a pipe. He was still living in the Infirmary while the staff attempted to get his seizures under better control. He wore a bandage around his head, but otherwise he seemed to be perfectly normal. He rose as Bea entered the room and greeted her with a shy smile. Sticking out his hand to shake hers, he said,

"I sure am glad to see you. I understand that you're the one who found me in the tunnel the other day. You probably saved my life and I've been wanting to thank you again. That was the second time you saved somebody — first Muley and then me."

As Bea shook his proffered hand and started to say something to minimize her part in the two rescues, she was gently interrupted by Miss Humphrey saying,

"She had to save your life, Glenn. We wouldn't be able to get along without you around here."

"I heard that you were busy saving the lives of the attendants during the tornado, too," added Glen to Bea.

With a blush, she answered,

"The truth is that trouble seems to follow me, and so far, the Lord has helped me to find a way out."

They all laughed at that and the conversation was once again interrupted. This time it was by the high pitched voice of another inmate who had wheeled herself over to the group in her wheelchair.

"Hello, Mother," she said to Miss Humphrey. "Who is this pretty lady? I'm Amelia Earhart. I'm an airplane pilot. I fly all over the world."

She directed this information toward Bea, who raised her eyebrows in amazement.

"Yea," drawled Glenn. "That's how you broke your arm, flying off the top of a wardrobe."

"That's not true." she retorted. "I crash landed in France. What do you know about it anyhow? You weren't there."

Miss Humphrey quickly intervened.

"Where did you get that nice, new wheelchair, Amelia?" she asked.

They decided that a famous person like me should be able to travel in class," came the answer. "The only problem is these safety belts they strap me in with. How am I ever going to keep up with my flying skills if they won't even let me get back into my plane?"

With that, she gave the restraints around her a strong tug but they wouldn't budge.

Miss Humphrey kindly explained to her that it was important for them to keep such a famous person safe while her broken arm healed, and then she turned to introduce Bea to the staff and other inmates on the ward.

Bea noticed Stephen Stephenson sitting in an overstuffed chair in the corner. He was an inmate from the J-Ward where she usually worked. She had been the nurse who had filled out the paper work for him to go to the dentist to have all of his teeth extracted. That decision had been made because Stephen was a biter. He had bitten himself and other people many times. The last time, his target had been Dr. Anderson. After that the extraction had been ordered without delay. He was heavily sedated now since he was usually hyperactive. His face was bruised and swollen, and he wore a bib to catch the blood tinged saliva drooling from his gums.

Stella Paquette paced by the nurses as they were discussing Stephen's condition. She had removed her shirt, but was swathed in bandages from waist to chin. She was recovering from a double mastectomy. Even though she was only eighteen years old, she had been very well endowed in the breast department and had become dangerous to the other inmates and staff because she had the behavior of stripping from the waist up and twirling her pendulous mammary appendages around, hitting people in the face with them. After giving several people black eyes, it was decided that the offending breasts must be removed.

One of the inmates who especially interested Bea was a beautiful teenager lying behind a screen on her bed in the corner of the females' sleeping area. She lay weeping into a handkerchief, head turned toward the wall. When Miss Humphrey tried to engage her in conversation, she would not respond, only turning away and crying harder. Miss Humphrey gently patted her back and left her alone, returning to where the charge nurse was writing in a file at the nurses' station.

As they discussed the girl in question, Bea learned that her name was Alice Nelson. She was the daughter of a well known politician in the State. She had been an outstanding student and popular in her school and community. Then, she had suddenly begun having grand mal seizures, for no apparent reason. During the seizures she had taken many hard falls, several times receiving bruises and lacerations on her lovely face. Her parents had taken her to all the best doctors, but had not been able to control the seizure activity.

Finally, in desperation, they had brought her to the Crystal Colony, believing that this would be the safest, most therapeutic environment for her to be in. She had been unhappy and unwilling to become a part of the Colony since her arrival about three months ago and had continued to have seizures and falls. She had another facial laceration during a seizure following the tornado and they had not been able to assuage her grief since.

As long as Bea and Miss Humphrey were on the West Ward, Amelia continually tailed them. It was difficult for them to converse between themselves or with others as she called out,

"Mother, Mother," and then shared loudly with them all her fantasies of past and future aerial exploits. Through it all Miss Humphrey and the other caregivers were patient and kind with her.

After leaving the West Ward, Bea asked for more information about Amelia. It was explained that her name was really Amelia Rice. She had been living at the colony for several years and knew most of the staff and inmates. It was true that she was an epileptic. However, she was also mentally ill, with delusions of grandeur and hallucinations of various kinds. It had been decided that her placement at Crystal Colony was probably a better one than if she had been sent to a facility for the mentally ill, so she had been placed here.

Miss Humphrey then explained that the North-Wing of the Infirmary was the home of some of the higher functioning female inmates. These were women who had jobs within the colony. They worked in the laundry, kitchen, garden, housekeeping, and in assisting in the physical care of lower functioning inmates.

The nurses took a short walk through the North-Ward. By this time most of the women had retired for the night because they were required to be up early in the morning to begin their duties. There was only one attendant on duty in that ward, just to make sure everything was alright and to report to the nurses on West-Ward if one of the inmates had a seizure or became sick or injured during the night.

Bea and Miss Humphrey left the Infirmary Building then and went out into the balmy, summer night to make rounds in the other buildings. Everywhere they went the staff and inmates treated Miss Humphrey with obvious love and respect. She answered their questions and calmed their fears as she moved graciously among them. Bea quickly noticed that every person with whom Miss Humphrey interacted received some kind of honest complement from her. It may be a new hairstyle, a lovely smile, a new skill learned, or a job well done. They were all made to feel valued by her in some way. As night fell, she was bringing warmth and sunlight into each life she touched.

Because so much time was taken up in orientation and explanation during the first rounds, by the time the nurses had returned to the Infirmary Building it was time to start rounds all over again. So, they did.

Everything was calm and quiet on the East-Wing.

However, when they arrived on the West-Wing, the nurses were obviously upset and so was Glenn. Apparently, it was a hard and fast rule that male and female inmates were not to have physical contact with one another, especially in the sleeping areas. But, one of the attendants had found Glenn sitting on the side of Alice Nelson's bed, cradling her in his arms while he rocked her, humming softly. Alice had fallen asleep in that position. When the attendant found them in this compromised situation, she had whispered to Glenn that he should lay Alice down and come out of the room immediately.

Glenn was irate because he felt he was being treated like a criminal for doing something kind and good for Alice. He kept saying that he was not doing anything wrong and that they should trust him more. The nurses were trying to explain to him that the rules were for his own good as well as all the other inmates and that he must learn to function within them. Miss Humphrey reinforced what the other nurses were telling Glenn, however she complemented him on his kind and generous heart and walked with him to his bed where he retired, his ruffled feathers somewhat smoothed.

Chapter 11

COFFEE WITH DOCTOR HECTOR

The rest of those rounds proved to be uneventful and when the nurses returned to the Infirmary Building again, they were both ready for a well earned break. As they entered the front door of the Infirmary Building, Miss Humphrey noticed a light in the Doctor's Office. She tapped tentatively on the office door and a deep voice called out,

"Come in."

Upon opening the door, the nurses were greeted with the sight of Doctor Hector sitting at his desk with an open medical journal lying before him. His auburn hair was tousled. His clothes were rumpled and he obviously needed a shave but his broad grin and cheery greeting made up for his untidy appearance.

"Hello, beautiful ladies," he said. "Come on in and share some coffee with me. As you probably know, I'm on call tonight and couldn't sleep, so I decided to come over here and do some research to see if I could find some answers for some of these out of control seizure patients."

He waved his big hand toward a stack of books and journals on his desk as he spoke.

Miss Humphrey returned his smile with her own unusual grin and responded playfully,

"How could we pass up an offer like that from such a neatly dressed, suave and debonair gentleman? I'll go get some cups."

Then she turned back into the hall and left Bea standing there beneath the doctor's gaze.

"Well, Miss Jenkins, I believe it is. You're looking very well considering what you have been through the past few days. Have a seat while I tell you that you are even more beautiful than the first time I laid eyes on you."

His eyes twinkled as Bea's face turned bright pink. She had no trouble remembering when he had first seen her in the treatment room of this very building after she had helped bring Glenn in for treatment. She knew it wouldn't take much to appear more beautiful than that.

"Don't be embarrassed," the doctor continued. "You were disturbingly lovely with those rags and combs falling out of your hair and blood all over you. I guess it would take a man with special training to recognize that though."

Bea was spared having to reply to his teasing by the reappearance of Miss Humphrey, bearing two clean coffee cups.

"And here comes the lady with the lamp," continued Doctor Hector. "If ever there was a personification of Florence Nightingale, this nurse comes the closest I have ever seen. Please help yourself to that liquid, black gold in the pot and have a seat on one of the doctor's thrones."

All smiles, Miss Humphrey filled a cup for Bea and took a seat in one of the desk chairs. Bea, feeling a little shy and uncomfortable, perched tentatively in the one remaining chair and glanced about the office as she sipped her coffee.

One wall of the office was lined with windows over-looking the lawn and flowerbeds in riotous bloom in the moonlight. A few houseplants grew in pots on the window-sills. Two of the walls were lined with bookshelves, reaching from ceiling to floor and filled with medical books and jour-nals. The doctors' desks were lined up like freight cars along the window wall. Most of them were neat and orderly, but Doctor Hector's was loaded with books, journals and papers in a disordered array. There was only room for a legal pad and a pen in the center of this chaos. It was obvious that the big red head had been laboring long and hard over his research.

"Have you made any great discoveries tonight?" queried Miss Humphrey.

That was all it took to launch the good doctor into a review of what he had been learning from all his research. He was still waxing eloquent an hour later when Miss Humphrey politely interrupted him to say that it was time for Bea and her to make their next rounds.

"And you had better get some sleep, Doc," she gently added, "You have a full day tomorrow and we don't want you to get sick."

He thanked them for their visit and with a gargantuan yawn, agreed that it was probably time for him to get some shut eye.

As the women hurried through their rounds this time they discussed what Doctor Hector had shared with them and Bea was able to ask some questions of Miss Humphrey that she had been embarrassed to ask the doctor.

"I have learned more about the symptoms and treatments of Epilepsy tonight than I did in all my training as a nurse," said Bea. "I had no idea that there was so much that was still unknown about the causes and treatment. It really makes me feel ignorant to hear all that you and Doctor Hector know about it."

"Doctor Hector has a special interest in Epilepsy," replied Miss Humphrey. "I wouldn't normally share medical information about a staff member with anyone else, but you need to know that he suffers from fits himself and you may be with him when he has one. That's how he got that scar on his forehead. He took a fall and hit his head on the sharp edge of a treatment table. That was before he came here to work, but after he had completed his medical training. I doubt if he would have been able to get into a medical school if he had a history of epilepsy when he applied. You know that people are discriminated against throughout our society if they are known epileptics. There are many people who believe that having fits means that one is demon possessed and/or mentally retarded. I'm afraid that it will take many years to make people accept the fact that fits are caused by a medical malfunction in the brain. In the meantime, people like you and me and Doctor Hector will just have to keep giving our love and support and understanding to the victims of this condition and keep looking for ways to treat and maybe cure or prevent epilepsy."

By seven o'clock Monday morning, Bea had learned so much about the staff, inmates, policies and procedures of the colony that she felt somewhat overwhelmed, but strangely warmed and invigorated and ready to continue on this adventure.

As she prepared for bed in the Wilkey's beautiful guest room, she thanked God for bringing her to a place where she could feel so needed and yet so nurtured by kind and gentle people.

Chapter 12

A SECRET TRYST

F reshly unfurled fern fronds rose majestically from the
forest floor which was littered with the welcoming faces
of millions of pink and white Trillium nestled in their bed
of emerald green leaves as the two stepped lightly among
them. A dappled pattern of lights and shadows played over
their bodies as they moved silently together through the cool
bower. Her delicate white hand and his large work hard-
ened one seemed to melt together as one. It was impossible
to tell where one hand ended and the other began. A gray
squirrel scolded as he scampered up a giant oak tree nearby.
The birds were silent in the canopy above except the distant
calls of crows as they warned of the presence of the couple.
An army of mosquitoes (called Minnesota's State Birds by
natives of the State) filled the air around them, mingling
with numerous honey bees, hummingbirds, colorful butter-
flies, and various other insects, all vying for the nectar of
the wild flowers growing in riotous profusion around them.
The oil of Lavender and Citronella they had applied before
entering the woods kept the majority of the insects from carrying the couple off for lunch.

The girl looked up from under the broad brim of her straw hat into his kind, tanned face with a mischievous twinkle in her eyes.

With a shy grin, in a whisper, he queried, "What's so funny now?"

"You look like an Arabian Sheik in that turban," she quietly giggled, covering her mouth with her free hand.

"Well, if you think this turban looks funny, you would really laugh if you could see the weird haircut and catgut decorations that are under it.. I think I'll get a nice hat of some kind to wear when the bandage comes off and they take out the stitches," with a soft chuckle, he quietly replied.

"What kind of hat do you think I would look good in?"

"Maybe you should wear an airplane pilot's helmet to protect your head in future falls, or better yet, you might look more sporting in a football helmet."

"I know you're just kidding, but that might not be a bad idea. I'll have to give that some serious thought. But, if I have to wear a helmet, then you will, too. Maybe we could make yours more feminine by dying it pink and adding some lace and blue ribbons to match your eyes," he added with another grin.

He stooped to select a large Trillium blossom, which he then tucked under the blue ribbon she had tied around the crown of her hat. The adoring look she gave him for that gesture was too irresistible for him, and he bent to meet her full lips with his. Time stood still as they lingered there with their arms wound around each other.

A twig snapped close by and they quickly broke the embrace and looked guiltily around. This startled the small, spotted fawn who had inadvertently come into their secret space. Its big eyes met theirs' briefly, and then bounded off among the trees to find the security of its mother.

The lovers looked at one another with mingled fear and guilt.

"What am I doing to you?" he asked with sincere concern as he saw the signs of fear and embarrassment on her countenance. "What am I doing to you?" he repeated as his shoulders slumped.

"There must be a way for us to be together without feeling so afraid and guilty," she answered. "It makes me angry to have to hide like this. We aren't doing anything wrong. I know that you love me, and I have never loved anyone but you. There must be a way." Tears sparkled in her eyes as she stomped her foot in anger and frustration in the moist leaves on the forest floor. "Something is just wrong with this system. We have to figure it out. I refuse to live like this any longer."

He took her tenderly into his arms and stroked her back as she trembled with indignation.

"Sweetheart, you know that if they found out about us we would both be punished with some kind of disciplinary action. What else can we do? I want you to be mine forever. I want you to be my wife and live with me on our own farm, in our own house, built with my own two hands, but this curse we have been placed under prevents us from living normal lives. We just have to go on snatching stolen moments together in secret and living in the fantasy of our minds until we die in the midst of a fit."

With that, the girl pushed him violently away from her and stepped back with her hands on her hips and a determined look he had never seen on her face before. She spoke in a firm, measured voice.

" I don't accept that," she said. "God is our Father, and He cares about us as his own children. The Bible says that He will give us our heart's desires if we ask Him, in Jesus' name. That's one thing we can do. I believe that God gave us this love for one another, and that it is His will for us to be together as husband and wife. I don't know how He will bring it about, but I am going to start believing that He will, and I want you to start believing that, too!"

As she stood thus, strong and defiant, a shaft of sunlight came slanting between the leafy roof above them and struck her full in the face. There was no doubt in his heart that this beautiful little woman was capable of the kind of faith that she professed and that she had faith that could indeed move mountains.

As she spoke, somehow the enormity of their plight lost some of its importance. *He thought to himself, as she stood thus before him, What a woman I have found. I don't deserve such an amazing woman She's small in stature, but she has the soul of a giant.*

"We will be together, in front of God and everybody. We will have that farm and that house. And, we will not have to hide anymore. I have to believe that. You have to believe that. Even if we both have to wear football helmets and mail armor, we will survive," she continued.

She stomped her foot again and shook her fist at the trees. Then she threw her arms around his neck and kissed him soundly.

"Now," she said as she broke softly from his returned embrace, "We'd better get back before we are missed. We'll continue to play their games until the Lord shows us how to solve this problem."

Chapter 13

BACK TO THE HOOT OWL SHIFT

A brand new nurse's cap was perched on Bea's freshly washed and curled hair when she arrived at the door of the Area Nurse's Office half an hour early on Saturday evening two weeks after her orientation to the hoot owl shift. Judith had presented the hat to her that afternoon when she came for a visit. She had said that Sister Anne at the convent had helped her make it and that they planned to make another, "In case this one flies away, too," she had added with a mischievous sparkle in her eyes.

Bea had been busy re-writing her report for Miss Peterson. She had asked Judith to read it and it had been pronounced, "impressive." Bea planned to deliver it when she went on duty that evening. The Director of Nursing had not mentioned it again after the tornado, but Bea considered it a duty to complete it and get it out of the way so it wouldn't feel like a weight hanging over her head.

Miss Peterson was already in the office completing her notes in the, <u>Daily Log Book</u>, when Bea arrived. She greeted Bea with a cheery, "HI there." Quickly completing the task at hand, she turned to Bea and gave her an oral report of changes and unusual happenings, which she would need to know for follow up over the next twelve hours. The most important item reported was the condition of Alice Nelson. She had suffered another grand mal seizure and had sustained another facial laceration. She was once again a patient in Infirmary-West and was deeply depressed. Otherwise, there were just the usual seizures, lacerations, and maladaptive behaviors to report on the other inmates throughout the colony.

Miss Peterson said that Dr. Irwin was on call tonight and Bea had already learned that he did not appreciate being called late at night unless there was a true emergency. That made her feel a little more unsure of herself, but didn't let the other nurse know of her fears. She knew that the night staff was extremely competent and would help her any way they could.

Bea handed her report to Miss Peterson as they were saying good night and Bea wasted no time beginning her rounds. Everything on the East Ward was under control and quiet. Judith had the night off, but Bea greeted the other workers and inmates cordially. Remembering Miss Humphrey's way of finding something to complement everyone, she congratulated the staff on the cleanliness and sweet fragrance of the ward and told Joy how lovely she looked. This was rewarded with an angelic smile before continuing to the West-Ward.

All was quiet on the West-Ward until Amelia noticed that Bea had arrived. When she did, she immediately wheeled her chair over to Bea and greeted her loudly.

"Hello, Pretty Nurse. You have a new hat on. That's really fancy. Where did you get that hat? I'd like to wear a hat like that if I wasn't an airplane pilot."

Then she launched into her usual spiel about her aviation adventures, following Bea around the ward and interrupting conversations Bea attempted to have with the staff. One of the attendants quickly realized the problem and distracted Amelia by asking her if she would like to take a ride outside. She agreed and they left through the back door with an uninterrupted train of chatter.

Nurse Brown was then able to tell Bea that Alice Nelson was sleeping. Dr. Irwin had ordered some Belladonna for her and she had finally fallen into a deep slumber.

Bea took a peek at the sleeping girl and, thanking Nurse Brown for the report, headed out to make her rounds on the other wards. She spent extra time on each ward trying to get to know the night staff and inmates better and reading charts where unusual situations caught her attention.

It was a beautiful evening and she enjoyed walking between the buildings breathing in the soft, Minnesota summer air and watching the birds, squirrels, and other wild life that shared the colony grounds.

She was greeted with respect and friendliness on all the wards, but when she arrived on B-Ward she was almost smothered by a huge hug from Mrs. Shipman. She and her husband were both on duty and she told everyone within her hearing that this was the nurse who had saved many lives during the tornado. Bea felt somewhat embarrassed by all this effusive praise and tried to downplay her part in the event, but Mr. Shipman backed up his wife's claims and she was pretty well squelched in her denials.

Mrs. Shipman plied her with cookies and iced tea, telling her that she was, "just too skinny," and needed to "put some meat on yer bones."

Bea giggled all the way to the next building thinking, *I guess I am skinny compared with her. She sure has changed her mind about me compared to the way she treated me the first day we met. I'm glad the Lord helped me to get on her good side. It wasn't much fun being on the outs with her. That's for sure."*

When Bea arrived on A-Ward where Glenn Schubert lived, the staff told her that he was still working in the barn, but that his seizures seemed to be well controlled now. They said that a football helmet had been ordered for him to wear to protect his head from further damage in case of another fall.

"What a good idea," she responded. Maybe we should think about getting one for some of the other epileptics here in the colony."

Alice Nelson came into her mind right away. *I wonder,* she mused.

Then remembering her experience in the tunnel the day she found Glenn in seizure, she suggested that someone should go to the barn to check on him if he wasn't back in a few minutes.

After taking so much extra time making her first rounds of the wards, she found that she had to begin her rounds again as soon as she returned to the Area Nurses' Office.

This time she spent less time making rounds and returned to the office in plenty of time to take a break. As she entered the Infirmary Building, she noticed that the door to the doctor's office was standing open and a light was on in there. As she passed, she glanced inside and was surprised to see Doctor Hector bending over books and papers on his desk. Hearing her footsteps, he looked up with his usual grin.

"Hello, Sunshine," he said. "How are things going out there?" and motioning toward the coffee pot, added, "Do you have time for some coffee with me?

She noticed that he didn't have the unkept appearance he had presented when she and Miss Humphrey had found him studying the first night of her orientation to the hoot owl shift. This evening he was neatly dressed in a white dress

93

shirt, a dark blue necktie and blue gabardine dress pants. His
black shoes were highly polished. He was clean shaved and
his hair was carefully combed.

Now, this is the way a doctor is suppose to look, she
thought to herself, as she returned his smile and answered.

"I'd like that. I'll go get a cup."

"Wait," he said. "I bought a cup for you. See, it has sun-
flowers on it. When I saw it at Olson's Department Store it
reminded me of you. Just have a seat and I will pour."

Rising, he motioned toward one of the chairs, filled the
new cup and presented it to Bea with a bow and a flourish.
She perched tentatively on the edge of the chair, accepting
the cup shyly with reddening cheeks and a timid,

"Thank you. You bought this cup just for me?"

"Yes. It reminded me of you and I thought you would like
it. We can keep it here in my desk drawer and you can use it
whenever you visit me. Is that alright?"

"That is very kind of you. I don't know what to say except,
thank you."

"That's all you need to say and you're very welcome. It is
my privilege." he answered.

"Isn't that a new cap you're wearing? I haven't seen you
wearing your cap before. It's such a pretty, feminine thing."

Bea was blushing again as she answered. "Thank you.
Yes, Judith and one of the Benedictine sisters at the convent
where she's staying, made it for me. Mine blew away in the
tornado. Wasn't that a thoughtful thing for them to do for
me? Everyone has been so kind to me since all my belong-
ings were blown away. I believe I have a nicer wardrobe now
than before. The Lord certainly is good to me."

The conversation continued as they began to get to know
one another on a personal level. He told her about his family
in New York. His grandfather, father and two older brothers
had been physicians before him and his mother was a nurse.

He chuckled as he said he was like a stray puppy away over here in Minnesota, since the rest of his family still lived and worked on the East Coast.

She told him about her father being killed in France during the Great World War, and how her mother and only brother had died with influenza during the epidemic in 1917. She said that her mother's parents, Grandmother and Grandfather Stretch, had taken her in and cared for her on their farm about forty miles from here, sacrificing to keep her in school through high school and then nurse's training.

Suddenly, Bea looked up at the clock on the wall and jumped up from her chair.

"Oh, my! I'm late for my next rounds. Thank you for the coffee and conversation. I really have to go!"

With that, she headed down the hall toward the East-Ward, on the run. Doctor Bradley Hector watched her retreat with a pensive expression and then slowly turned back to his books, but found that he was unable to concentrate on them. Rising slowly, he poured himself another cup of coffee and began to pace back and forth in the office, occasionally stopping to stare out the open window at the darkening sky.

The West-Ward was quiet when Bea arrived this time. Alice Nelson was still sleeping and Amelia Rice had joined her in Slumber Land. The rest of the rounds were uneventful except that the staff on A-Ward said that they were becoming concerned about Glenn and had sent one of the men to the barn to check on him. Bea asked them to call the West-Ward when they located him.

Upon returning to the Infirmary Building, Bea found Doctor Hector standing in the open door of the doctor's office waiting for her. He told her that he had forgotten to tell her that he had taken call for Doctor Irwin tonight and if she had any problems, she should not hesitate to call him.

"I never seem to tire of hearing your voice," he added.

"By the way, what hours will you be working this Wednesday?"

"The day shift," she answered. Why do you ask?"

"I was wondering if I could escort you to prayer meeting in the Chapel. It begins at seven-thirty and we may be a few minutes late, but the Chaplain is used to some of us coming in a little late. What do you think?"

Bea was so surprised by this invitation, she was speechless for a moment. Then, regaining her composure somewhat, answered,

"I guess that would be alright."

"Good," said the tall redhead.

"I'll come to Wilkey's for you at seven-thirty. Alright?"

"Alright?" answered Bea, with a nod and a blush.

"Very good," responded the doctor.

"I'm going to go home and try to get some shut eye now. Mondays are always hectic. Don't hesitate to call me if you need me though."

"Alright, Bea said again. "Good night. Sweet Dreams."

"I'm sure they will be," he answered and turned to lock the office door.

Bea watched him leave the Infirmary Building before she turned toward the East Ward again. She wasn't running or walking now. She was sure she was floating. She could hardly believe what had just happened. Doctor Hector had just asked her to go to Prayer Meeting with him.

"I can't believe it," she said to herself. "He's so nice and so smart and sooo tall."

Chapter 14

MISSING

───⟪ ⟫───

B ea was beginning her four A.M. rounds in the East-Ward when running footsteps were heard coming down the hall. Carol Smith came rushing onto the ward, black hair flying, and a look of panic on her face.

"She's gone! Alice is gone! She gasped, breathlessly.

"She's nowhere on the ward and I've looked all around the building! I can't find her anywhere!"

Bea ran toward the West-Ward with her.

"We'll look for her on the ward again. Maybe she's found a new place to hide," she told Carol, in as calm a voice as she could muster under the circumstances.

The other workers on the ward were not at all calm when they arrived there, however.

Mrs Brown said, "There's a call for you from A-Ward," as she handed Bea the telephone receiver.

The caller did nothing to ease Bea's mind. He said that Glenn had not yet been found and that a horse was missing from the barn. As Bea was receiving this information, she saw the caregivers on West-Ward going over every inch of the place, searching for Alice or some clue where she might have gone. She thanked the caller and told him to continue

97

the search for Glenn and that she would make some calls to get more help.

As soon as the call was complete, she called Doctor Hector. His sleepy voice came on the line after just one ring. She told him that Glenn and Alice were both missing and asked him for his advice on the next thing she should do.

He said that he would be right over and to call Dr. and Mrs. Anderson and Miss Peterson.

Mrs Anderson answered the phone and said that she and her husband would come right away, but that Bea should call Miss Peterson and then the sheriff. By the time Bea had made those two calls, Drs. Anderson and Hector and Mrs. Anderson were already on West-Ward. A search plan was put immediately into operation. A long blast was sounded on the steam whistle from the Boiler Room to warn of an emergency. A communication base was set up in Dr. Anderson's office in the Main Building. All off duty employees were called in, as well as all the sheriff's deputies and volunteer firemen. It was explained to everyone that the inmates who were missing were both at high risk for seizures and falls and that the girl had been threatening suicide. Men and women spread out in all directions carrying various kinds of lanterns and lights to guide the way.

Doctor Anderson took the responsibility of calling Alice's parents in Saint Paul. State Senator Nelson said that they would come as quickly as possible. It would take at least an hour and a half for him and his wife to drive to the colony.

Chapter 15

THE LOST IS FOUND

A large gray horse and rider moved wraith like on a dear trail along the bank of the Brandy River in the pre-dawn darkness. The man sat tall in the saddle with his straw hat pulled low over his forehead to protect his face from overhanging branches. Though the animal and man were both familiar with the trail, each step was taken carefully because it was so dark and recent rains had made the way wet and slippery. The rider was deep in thought, letting the horse find his own way over the sodden trail when suddenly, the horse shied away from a shape lying half in and half out of the water. At first the rider thought that it was a piece of driftwood washed up on the bank by the high water. But upon closer inspection, he realized that it was a scantily dressed human and he quickly dismounted for a closer look.

"Dear Lord!" he muttered. "It's Alice!"

The beautiful girl lay silent and unmoving. She was barefoot and wearing only her nightgown. Bending low, the man felt for a pulse and listened for sounds of breathing.

"Alice, can you hear me?"

There was no answer, but he quickly determined that she had a faint pulse and shallow respirations. Her body was icy cold to his touch, so he quickly removed the saddle blanket from the horse, and wrapping it around the limp body, he draped Alice over the horse's withers. Leaping back into the saddle, he took the reigns and spoke softly.

"Get up, Shadow. You'll have to be careful, but we need to get her back to the colony as fast as we can."

The horse seemed to understand the urgency in his friend's voice and picked up the pace. The man bent low over his precious cargo, trying to use his own body heat to help get her warm. Glancing up he saw lights, dozens of them, moving across the fields and into the woods.

"They must have discovered that she was missing and have come to look for her," he murmured to Shadow.

The horse had cleared the slippery path and trees along the river and had found sure footing on the pasture path, so was urged to a trot by the rider. As he came to within hearing distance to the first person with a light, he called out.

"Were you looking for Alice Nelson? I found her down by the river."

"Is that you, Glenn?" yelled the searcher.

"Yes. She's hurt and unconscious. I'm taking her directly to West-Ward."

The searchers began calling to one another down the line of lights and before Glenn reached the Infirmary Building, a long blast was heard from the steam whistle on the boiler. This was the pre-arranged signal that the lost had been found. Shadow and his passengers were met by the West Wing staff, who worked together to lift Alice carefully from the horse and carry her back to be placed on her bed. One of the farm workers took Shadow back to the stable to be watered and bedded down after Glen had dismounted to help with the limp and unresponsive patient.

In a matter of seconds, Alice was surrounded with all the doctors on the staff and most of the nurses. The West-Ward was in turmoil. All of the searchers were milling around outside the back door and the inmates on the ward had all been aroused by the noise and excitement.

Dr. and Mrs. Anderson and Miss Peterson quickly gave instructions to the staff and volunteers. On duty staff were told to take care of the other inmates and everyone else was sent to the dining room in the Main Building if they wanted to stick around to find out how Alice was doing.

Glenn felt a tap on his shoulder and turned to find the sheriff beside him.

"You will need to come with me, young man," he said. "We have some questions for you."

Sure," he answered. "Anything I can do to help." The rest of the morning was filled for Bea with a blur of helping with the examinations, X-rays, laboratory tests, and written reports for Alice. Bea completely forgot about Glenn as she was immersed in the business of evaluating, treating and making written records on Alice's chart. The doctors and nurses worked together in a smoothly functioning team, using all the skills and training they had to try to save her life. Before long, it was decided that Alice had a scalp laceration and a possible brain concussion. She was also suffering from exposure. Even though it had been a warm night, the river water had been cold and she had been lying partially immersed in it.

At least her condition was stable when Bea was finally able to wind up her paper work and report off to Miss Peterson at almost nine o'clock.

Bea was so tired by then that it took all she could do to stay awake on the way back to the Wilkey's with Inga driving the buggy. She didn't take the time to eat anything when she got home. She just went into her room, shut the door, kicked off her shoes, threw her cap onto the dresser, and sprawled out on the bed without even taking off her uniform.

Chapter 16

REPRIEVE

—⸨⸩—

Senator Nelson and his wife, Marie arrived at the colony at nine-thirty that morning and went directly to the Infirmary Building. There they saw their daughter lying unresponsive in the bed with her head wrapped in bandages. This was not the first time they had observed her in this condition, but it never ceased to bring tears to their eyes when they witnessed this symbol of her suffering. She lay, so pale and motionless that it seemed that she was already dead. The helplessness and seeming hopelessness of the situation weighed heavily on their hearts.

Rage filled the brain of the senator. This man had power to direct the activities of thousands of people. He had millions of dollars at his disposal, and yet had not enough power nor finances to solve his beautiful daughter's problems.

As Senator Nelson turned from Alice's bed, he almost bumped into Dr. Irwin, who had come in and was standing quietly behind the couple.

Oh, hello, Doctor. I didn't see you there. What is her prognosis?" asked the father.

"We don't know yet," answered the old man.

"Her vital signs are stable now, but she doesn't respond to stimuli yet. She may come out of it or she may not. There's just no way for us to know right now."

"How in the (expletive) did this happen?"the grieving man asked angrily.

"I am really unsure of the answer to that question," replied the doctor.

"The West-Ward staff said that she was apparently sleeping in her bed when they checked her at three o'clock, but was gone when they made their rounds at four. They immediately sounded the alarm and a search was undertaken at that time. Searchers were just spreading out to look for her when another inmate, Glenn Schubert came riding from the direction of the river on a horse with her, saying he had found her unconscious on the river bank."

"What was he doing down by the river on a horse at that hour?"

"Well, he works on the farm and has access to all the animals. The sheriff has been questioning him, but he won't tell anyone why he was out by the river then. Some people suspect that he was meeting Alice there for a romantic tryst, or had actually kidnapped her and taken her there against her will. I know him pretty well and don't believe either of those scenarios. They have him locked in a seclusion room in the Main Building now."

"I want to talk to that man right now," stated the senator, drawing himself up to his most imposing stance. This was not very tall since he was somewhat vertically challenged. However, he had a way of puffing himself up to the appearance of a very powerful opponent when the occasion arose.

"Come on," he continued as he took Marie by the arm and hurried from the room, leaving the doctor without even a thank you.

Upon arriving in the Main Building, the senator and his wife marched directly to Dr. Anderson's office and entered without knocking.

"Oh, hello, Senator," said the administrator, rising quickly from his desk and holding out his hand in greeting.

Grasping the outstretched hand for a quick, perfunctory touch, the senator responded.

"Where is this Glenn Schubert?" I am going to ask him some questions, and I <u>will</u> get some answers."

Dr. Anderson's hair began to move back and forth on his head as he answered in soothing, placating tones.

"We have him in seclusion and the sheriff has been questioning him. I'm sure that he will tell us the whole story after he has a few hours to think about it. He has always been a kind, trustworthy and dependable inmate since he came here and has never ever given us any trouble."

"A few hours, my foot!" exploded the little senator, stamping the afore mentioned appendage.

"I shall talk with him right now! Take me to him!"

The doctor's scalp was moving with great vigor as he moved quickly toward his office door.

"Yes. Yes. Please come with me."

The trio moved down the hall in a very military like fashion, down the stairs and then down that hallway to the door of the seclusion room. The doctor drew out a key, opened the heavy metal door and stepped aside to allow the politician to enter.

As Marie started to follow her husband into the room, he said,

"No! I'll speak with him alone."

She obediently backed out and the doctor closed the door and locked it. The two of them stood in the hall trying to hear what was being said, but heard only low murmuring for several minutes. Then there was a knock on the door and Dr.

Anderson once more turned the key in the lock and the portal swung wide open.

Glenn stood tall beside the diminutive gentleman in the doorway. The senator spoke.

"Glenn is innocent of any wrong doing. He saved my daughter's life and I will be forever grateful to him. Sometime in the very near future you will be told why he was on horseback down by the river this morning, but not just yet. Please accept my word on this for now, Doctor."

Dr. Anderson nodded in acquiescence as he led the way back upstairs to his office. At that point Glenn asked,

"May I please go to work now?"

Senator Nelson answered for the doctor.

"Of course, Son, but get some breakfast first," he said with a smile and a pat on Glenn's arm.

Dr. Anderson shrugged his shoulders and agreed.

"Of course, Glenn. Don't forget to wear your helmet."

As Glenn headed for his room at a trot, Senator Nelson turned to the doctor and gave him a sincere handshake and a smile as he commended him.

"You're doing a fine job, Doctor. I appreciate your consideration and cooperation. Now, let's see what we can do for that little girl of ours."

Offering his wife his arm, they strolled back to the West Ward at a more leisurely pace, leaving Doctor Anderson staring at the office door with a puzzled frown and a very lively scalp.

Chapter 17

THE MIRACLE

O n the following Wednesday morning, as usual, Bea
came early to work on J-Ward. She had heard by way
of the nurse's grapevine that Alice Nelson was still unresponsive and that Glenn Schubert had been released from
custody and further questioning by Alice's father. Everyone
was speculating as to what had actually transpired on the
night of Glenn and Alice's disappearance. Most thought that
there was connection between the two. However, Senator
Nelson seemed to be convinced that Glenn was blameless,
so the work on the Colony Farm continued as if nothing had
happened.

Bea found an envelope from Miss Peterson addressed
to her on the bulletin board in the Nurse's Office. It con-
tained a commendation for the excellent report which she
had written on the happenings with Muley, Glenn Schubert,
and the escaped inmate car thieves. The nursing director said
that Dr. Anderson was also pleased with the report and with
Bea's performance of her duties since those adventures. They
were also very impressed with the meticulous way she had
written her nurse's notes since then. This really started the

day off great for Bea and after breathing a prayer of thanksgiving, she began her rounds on J-Ward.

The day went fairly smooth, with only one broken window, two minor lacerations, and one attempt by Jimmy Burdette to eat a centipede.

The one thing which kept bubbling up inside her, making her want to smile and giggle was the thought that she had a date with Dr. Hector to go to prayer meeting that night. It felt to her as if the end of the shift would never get there. She had talked with Judith last evening and had found out that she would be there also, as she was the regular pianist for the prayer services.

Bea had taken Inga and Mrs. Wilkey into her confidence regarding the impending date with the tall red headed doctor and the maid was waiting at the door of Cottage–Two at five minutes before seven so Bea could get home and change clothes before her escort called for her. Nellie, Wilkey's carriage horse was not used to being driven fast and was acting somewhat spooky when Inga cracked the whip to make her speed up on the way home. But years of practice with farm horses in Sweden helped Inga keep control of her and they made good time. Clothes, shoes, and hair ribbons were flying as Mrs. Wilkey helped Bea change into a pink crepe dress and pulled her hair up into a Martha Washington up-sweep, set off by a small rose colored bow. When the doorbell rang, the young nurse looked as if she had been making preparation for the appointment for several hours instead of a few minutes.

Bea's cheeks were pink and her eyes sparkled from exertion and excitement when she greeted her date and they headed out for the colony in his new silver/gray, one horse shay. His horse was a beautiful high stepping gray filly with white markings. Her name was, Princess and she was well trained. Doctor Hector was dressed in his Sunday best, with suit, tie, top hat, and spats. It was a beautiful summer evening. Flowers were blooming. Bees were buzzing and it seemed that all was right with their world.

Upon their arrival at the colony, the doctor helped Bea down from the buggy and tied Princess to a hitching post near the side door of the Main Building. They entered and descended the stairs to the basement where the chapel was to be found. They could hear soft piano music before they even entered. Judith sat before the instrument playing, "Father, Like A Shepherd Lead Us." The music was almost as beautiful as the lovely girl who was producing it. Her fingers seemed to caress, rather than strike the keys and her body swayed slightly in time to the rhythm. It seemed as if she and the piano were one.

Looking about her as the doctor seated her, Bea noted that the congregation consisted about half and half staff and inmates. The service began with another hymn during which everyone joined in. The singing was not altogether harmonious, since there were a few monotones in the group and not everyone could read, nor even speak coherently. However, what was lacking in quality was more than made up for in quantity. They certainly made a joyful noise as they sang, "Joyful, Joyful, We Adore Thee."

Father Royce then prayed an opening prayer. When he said his, "Amen.," it was echoed by several of the inmates, loudly and in unison.

With a smile, the chaplain then asked David Lance, a high level inmate to read from Psalm 61.

Hear my cry, O God attend to my prayer.
From the end of the earth I will
cry unto you,
When my heart is overwhelmed;
Lead me to the rock that is higher than I.
For you have been a shelter for me, and a
strong tower from my enemy,

I will abide in Your tabernacle forever;
I will trust in the shelter of Your wings.

For some reason this Psalm seemed to be especially meaningful to all those in attendance and many of them had misty eyes as the reader finished. The Psalm was followed by a short homily by the chaplain. He spoke briefly about the fact that God has promised His people a shelter when thy feel overwhelmed. He then gave the example of the recent incident, which had happened with Alice Nelson and suggested that they all say a special prayer for her.

Then he said, "In closing, let us all say the 'Lord's Prayer,' together followed by a few moments of silent prayers for Alice."

As people were beginning to exit, Bea spoke up saying, "May I have your attention, please. I believe that the Holy Spirit is leading me to ask you all to go with me over to the West Ward to lay hands on Alice and pray for her there."

Then turning to Father Royce she added,

"Will you please bring some Holy Water or Healing Oil and come with us, Reverend?"

Everyone looked at one another and then nodded in agreement as the chaplain replied,

"Of course. I'll meet you all over there."

He hurried down the hall toward his office as the rest of them followed Bea and Dr. Hector. They walked hand in hand toward the Infirmary Building. As they walked, Bea looked back to see how many were following and was pleased to see that most of the people who had been in the prayer meeting were coming, with Glenn Schubert bringing up the rear.

The priest had caught up with the rest of the group as they gathered around Alice's bed on the West Ward. Dr. Hector explained to the ward staff what was happening and the group parted to allow Father Royce to come to the head of Alice's bed. She lay completely still with closed eyes, as if in a deep sleep. Her color had improved and her breathing appeared normal. The attendants had dressed her in a sky blue gown which her mother had brought her. Although the hair on the top of her head had been shaved to clean the area of her laceration, they had brushed what was left to a glossy sheen hanging down around her shoulders.

As she had watched her grandparents do many times in the past, Bea now gave instructions to all present.

"Everyone come close and place a hand on Alice or her bed. Hold your other hand toward Heaven and as the Reverend anoints her head, we will all say a prayer for her, asking God to heal her completely."

Everyone followed her instructions and most of them began to pray aloud as the Priest began his prayer in Latin.

Even some of the lower level inmates who were unable tospeak in normal language began to babble in their own way. As they prayed, some of them had tears streaming down their cheeks. This continued for only a few minutes when one of the attendants said,

"Look! She's moving her head!"

Alice's blue eyes began to blink and she looked around her in confusion.

Father Royce said in amazement,

"Dear Lord!"

Bea and Dr. Hector said in unison,

"Praise the Lord!"

There were no dry eyes around that bed as Alice sat up and looked at everyone. They were all hugging one another and slapping one another on the back saying things like,

"It worked!"

"She's healed!"

"Praise God!"

Some were laughing and crying at the same time.

Bea went to the head of the bed and placing her arms around Alice, she said into her ear,

"The Lord has heard our prayers and healed you, Alice. You are going to be all right. He must have a special mission for you on this earth because He has given you back to us.

Alice pushed Bea forcefully away from her and fell back to her pillow. Turning her face to the wall she wailed,

"But I wanted to die! I wanted to die!"

She began to weep and moan, loudly.

A silence fell over the crowd in the room and the Charge Nurse quietly asked them to leave. Everyone filed out except Glenn Schubert, who stepped to the head of the bed and placing his hands on her shoulders, he gently said with a shaking voice,

"I could never let you die, Little Sister. You must know that we need you. I could never let you die."

With that, she sat back up and threw her arms around his neck. Burying her face in his chest she cried uncontrollably. He sat on the side of the bed, holding her and rocking back and forth as a parent would rock a child. As he rocked he kept saying in a singsong voice,

"It'll be all right, Little sister. It's going to be all right."

After several minutes her weeping quieted, but she continued to cling to him as she snuffled every few seconds. Finally, she said in a teeny tiny voice,

"Why aren't I dead? I went to the river to drown myself. The last thing I remember is stepping into the water. Why didn't I drown? I really wanted to die, Glenn."

With that, she tipped her head back and looked him directly in the face. What she saw was a face filled with suffering and covered with tears.

"That is where I found you. You must have slipped on the muddy bank and fell, hitting your head on a rock. Shadow and I brought you back here and you've been lying uncon- scious for many hours," he answered.

"Oh please, don't say you want to die. You can bring sun- shine to us all. This old world needs you so much. Just think, tonight all the people who came to prayer meeting came over here to pray for your healing and our prayers were answered. God must have a very special plan for your life. I'm just sure of it."

"But how can I go on having those fits and falling all over the place, soiling myself and cutting my face and head all up, Glenn? I just can't go on like that. I just can't."

Then she buried her face in his chest again and resumed her weeping.

"Aw, come on, Little Sister, you know that I have the same problem that you have but I have to rely on Jesus to see me through. He has promised to give us strength for each day and to help carry our load when it becomes to heavy for us. And look here, we could get you a helmet like mine and decorate it with pretty flowers or ribbons or somethin' an' you will be the Belle of the Ball. It would set a new fashion trend for the other girls here at the Crystal Colony an' they would all compete to see who has the prettiest helmet. We could even hold a beauty contest, an' you could be the judge. Besides that, I have been fallin' and floppin' around for more years than you an' lookit how handsome I am." (With his heightened emotions, he had lapsed back into the Tennessee accent he had grownup with as a child.)

This idea, presented with an encouraging smile, made her smile back. As the idea became clear in her mind, she let out a little giggle. Glenn chuckled back to her and before they knew it they were both convulsed in full blown laughter.

During this whole dialog, the West-Ward Charge Nurse, along with Bea, Dr. Hector, Father Royce, and Judith had been standing on the other side of the privacy screens sur- rounding Alice's bed, holding hands with one another, listening, and praying silently with tear streaked faces. With the sounds of laughter, smiles broke out all around and they all took deep sighs of relief. Glenn had once again saved the day.

Chapter 18

DREAMS FULFILLED

———⟨•/•/•⟩———

The church bells were ringing in the tower of Christ Our
Lord Church in River Ridge, Minnesota, on the second
Saturday evening on October of nineteen-twenty-four. The
full moon had already risen and shone down on the congre-
gentes moving joyfully up the wide stairs and through the
heavily carved wooden doors into the sanctuary as a soft,
warm breeze showered them with brilliantly colored leaves
from the surrounding maples, elms, oaks, and aspens. Inside,
some of them briefly stopped to dip their fingers into the Holy
Water, genuflect, and make the sign of the cross before following an usher to their assigned pew, where they repeated
the bow and crossing before being seated. Others, seemed a
bit uncomfortable with these rituals and simply followed the
usher to their place and sat, looking about as if in discovery
of an unfamiliar, but beautiful environment. The sanctuary
was lit with scores of candles and decorated with hundreds of
colored leaves and fall flowers. The candlelight danced and
shimmered on the stained glass windows, the gold and silver
altar appointments and the statuary lining the walls.

It was an unusual and eclectic gathering made up of
people of all social classes, educational status, varying ages

and levels of health and wealth. Probably most notable in their dress was the great number of people wearing padded, leather football helmets. The men and boys wore either plain black or brown. However, the females had modified their helmets in very unique and fanciful ways. Most of them had been painted to match the colors of their dresses. The use of feathers, jewels, and other bits of whimsy were all evident, limited only by their imaginations. Even Marie Nelson, the senator's wife sailed sedately down the aisle, her white gloved hand on the arm of the usher with the ultimate of fashionable millinery topping her golden hued helmet.

The choir was made up of Benedictine Sisters, all in traditional white and black habits. They were softly singing Psalms in lovely harmonies, accompanied on the organ by a beautiful young lady with long blond locks hanging in waves from around the edges of her beautifully decorated helmet. Father Royce came to the platform in his most festive vestments topped off with a shiny black helmet. He turned to bow, make the sign of the cross and say a quiet prayer before the alter.

As he turned back to face the congregation, the groom and best man entered together from the side door. Both men were dressed in three piece black suits, spats and matching helmets.

Mrs. Wilkey stood next to the organ and, lifting her violin to her chin began to play, accompanied by the organist. The ushers came from the back of the sanctuary, unrolling a white carpet down the center aisle to the front.

A tall, willowy, maid of honor was next to enter down the center aisle. She was wearing a soft, flowing, rust orange colored, velvet gown and carried a basket of multicolored chrysanthemums. She exchanged glowing smiles with everyone at the front.

At this point, the music changed to a more playful mood as the ring bearer came down the aisle carrying a white satin pillow onto which the rings had been tied with ribbons. Then, very slowly came the little, raven haired flower girl carrying a small replica of the basket in the hands of the maid of honor. She carefully scattered marigolds and colored leaves on the carpet as if that was the most important thing anyone had ever done before. Upon arrival at the front, the children joined hands and stood very close to the Maid of Honor, who smiled benevolently down at them and whispered,

"Very good job."

The music again changed to the "Wedding March," as the bride started down the aisle on the arm of Senator Nelson. She was dressed in white velvet with a velvet covered helmet over which a long lace veil draped over her head and shoulders.

The senator was outfitted with a formal black tuxedo with tails. He also wore a helmet to match his tux.

The congregation stood as the couple stepped in slow dignity over the flower strewn white carpet. The two were almost matched in height and she held tightly to his arm until they reached the front.

The ceremony was beautiful and solemn, at the end of which, Father Royce had the newly-weds face the congregation and announced,

"May I present Mr. and Mrs. Glenn and Judith Schubert."

Everyone stood and applauded as Glenn and Judith ran back up the aisle together, followed by Bea, on the arm of Dr. Bradley Hector. Natalie Ward, hand in hand with Timmy Larson came next followed by the smiling priest.

The music of choir and instruments swelled as the congregation was ushered out to the receiving line. Alice Nelson, at the organ played with joy and energy with a happy flush on her cheeks. She had not had a seizure since her friends had prayed for her healing and it had been decided that she could now move back to her parents' home in Saint Paul.

Considering how many epileptics had attended the wedding, it was a miracle that no one had a seizure during the entire service.

EPILOGUE

B ea and Bradley sat relaxing at the kitchen table of the big farmhouse, looking out the windows at the pasture and barn. Glenn sat at the head of the table as Judith served coffee and home made oatmeal cookies. The fire burned warmly in the range and a kitten played with the puppy's tail as they skidded about on the new, yellow and white, linoleum floor.

Glenn was saying,

"The Lord has sure been good to us. Just think, if I hadn't been over to the convent to visit Judith that night, I wouldn't have found Alice. And, if her father had not believed me and decided to reward me with this farm, Judith and I wouldn't have had enough money to get married. And, if we had not prayed for Alice's healing, she wouldn't have been able to go back home to live. And, if you, (looking at Dr. Bradley Hector,) hadn't studied and searched for new treatments for epilepsy, Judith and I wouldn't have as much control over our seizures and it wouldn't be safe for us to live outside the Colony."

"Well, praise the Lord!" interjected Bee,
and they all responded with a resounding,
"Amen!"